ISRAEL IN PROPHECY

by

JOHN F. WALVOORD

President, Dallas Theological Seminary

ZONDERVAN PUBLISHING HOUSE
GRAND RAPIDS, MICHIGAN

Printed in the United States of America

FOREWORD

This volume embodies a series of lectures delivered before the faculty, student body, and Oregon and Washington ministers on the campus of Western Conservative Baptist Theological Seminary, Portland, Oregon. Each year a lecturer is brought to the Seminary to lecture in his field of specialization on the Bueermann-Champion Lecture Foundation, which was established as a joint memorial to the Rev. Frederic Bueermann, an honored Baptist minister of the Northwest, and John B. Champion, M.A., B.D., minister, professor, scholar, and author. These lectures represent the fifteenth in the annual series.

The title, "Israel in Prophecy," covers the major prophecies relating to Israel as a nation and its obvious place in Biblical theology as a whole. Throughout, the premillennial aspect of the Lord's return is brought into clear relief based upon the unconditional fulfillment of the Abrahamic covenant promise to the elect nation of Israel. Confessedly, this presentation deals with an absorbingly interesting, controversial phase of Biblical prophecy, upon which much has been written, but which, in these discourses, is treated in the author's characteristic skillful and praiseworthy manner, a model in legitimate religious controversy.

The lecturer's recent visit to the sacred land, where the people of the land are again the recognized nation of Israel, furnished interesting sidelights of unique interest pertinent to the subject under discussion.

This publication is in response to the unanimous request on the part of the hearers, and we bespeak for this volume a spiritually-discerning and prayerful reading.

ALBERT G. JOHNSON
President, Western Conservative Baptist Seminary

Portland, Oregon

PREFACE

The establishment of the new state of Israel in the Middle East in 1948 introduced a new and important factor in the interpretation of Biblical prophecy. For generations the question of a future restoration of Israel has been debated. Some who saw no future for Israel expressed doubt that the nation would ever return to its native land. Others on the basis of Biblical prophecies predicted that some day Israel would be restored and would possess the Promised Land.

The day has come when expositors of Biblical prophecy no longer need to depend entirely on the prophetic Word for their hope of Israel's restoration. Before the eyes of the entire world the seemingly impossible has occurred. A people scattered for almost two millenniums are now firmly entrenched in the land of their forefathers. Regardless of theological point of view, all the world must acknowledge the partial restoration of the nation Israel and with it the revival of Israel's culture and religion. The growing economic importance of the nation as well as its recognition as a political state are now facts of history. No one today can say that a return of the nation of Israel is an impossibility. Under such circumstances, a restudy of Biblical prophecy relating to Israel is more than an academic or theological exercise, and it is a natural outgrowth of a contemporary situation.

From the standpoint of Biblical doctrine, the divine program for Israel can justly claim a place of central importance. Most of the Bible from the early chapters of Genesis to the concluding chapters of Revelation either directly or indirectly relate to the nation Israel. The understanding of Israel's program affects the interpretation of every book of the Bible. It is not too much to say therefore that a proper understanding of divine revelation relating to Israel is one of the most important and crucial issues in theology today.

Unfortunately, the study of the future of Israel has been obscured by controversy in other areas of Biblical theology. Liberal or neo-orthodox theologians, who do not accept the infallibility of the Scriptures, tend to ignore what the Bible teaches about Israel. Among conservatives there is also a radical division concerning the meaning of Biblical revelation in relation to Israel. Some contemporary amillenarians deny any future to Israel as such and consider the promises to Israel as being fulfilled in the church in the present age. Others believe that there will be a spiritual restoration of Israel, but tend to disregard the geographic and political aspects of Israel's promises. In the light of recent developments and the fact of a partial restoration of Israel in our day, it seems only reasonable to reconsider the time-honored interpretations of the Bible which anticipated such a restoration.

Because of the strategic and timely character of a restudy of the Biblical doctrine of the eschatology of Israel, it was a pleasure to accept the gracious invitation from the Western Conservative Baptist Theological Seminary at Portland, Oregon, to deliver a series of seven lectures developing this doctrine. The kind reception on the part of faculty and student body as well as visiting pastors from Washington and Oregon prompted the publication of the lectures.

In order to achieve a comprehensive study of prophecy relating to Israel within the limitations of seven lectures, it has been necessary to confine the discussion to major aspects of the doctrine. No attempt has been made to discuss hundreds of individual prophecies related to the nation Israel which in many cases have already been fulfilled. Quotations from the vast amount of literature available have also been necessarily kept to a minimum. The discussion has centered in Biblical exposition rather than in a comparison of works and ideas of theological and Biblical scholars. To help those who want to study the subject further, a selected bibliography is provided in addition to the topical and Biblical indices.

The goal of the lectures was to set forth the history and prophetic future of Israel in its broad outlines. The author is well aware of the fact that an exhaustive treatise on this subject would demand a volume many times the size of this study. A concise presentation, however, has many advantages. The reader is brought quickly to the crux of each issue without laborious consideration of details which really do not affect the outcome. It is hoped that the lectures as published will constitute a constructive contribution to Biblical interpretation, useful both for the novice and for the advanced scholar.

J. F. W.

CONTENTS

ISRAEL IN PROPHECY

Chapter I

THE NEW STATE OF ISRAEL

When Theodor Herzel announced in 1897 the purpose of the Zionist movement — "to create for the Jewish people a home in Palestine secured by public law" — few realized how dramatic would be the fulfillment. The Jews had dreamed for centuries of re-establishing themselves in their ancient land. Now this longing was translated into action. Few nations could point to a richer heritage as a basis for the hope of the restoration of the nation.

The History of Israel in the Old Testament

The history of Israel began more than thirty-five hundred years ago, when, according to the early chapters of Genesis, the divine call was extended to Abraham to leave his ancient land of Ur and proceed to a land that God would show him. After some delay, Abraham finally entered the land, and there the promised son Isaac was born.

Though God miraculously fulfilled the promise of a son in Isaac, Abraham himself never possessed the Promised Land but lived as a pilgrim and stranger. Rich in earthly goods, Abraham never fulfilled his hope of a homeland in his lifetime. His son Isaac shared a similar fate. Under Jacob, Isaac's son, the people of Israel forsook the Promised Land entirely and at the invitation of Joseph set up their homes in Egypt where they lived for hundreds of years. It was not until their very existence was threatened in Egypt by a hostile king that the day finally came for Israel's possession of the land. With Moses as their appointed leader, they began their momentous migration, one of the largest ever undertaken by any nation. After forty years of wandering in the wilderness, they finally completed their pilgrimage from Egypt to the land promised Abraham.

The book of Joshua records the conquest of Palestine and its partial occupation. The nation Israel, however, was doomed to generations of oppression and moral declension. They periodically were oppressed by Gentile nations about them with occasional cycles of spiritual and political revival, led by judges whom God raised up. The political anarchy which characterized the period of the judges was succeeded by the reign of the kings, beginning with Saul, and was followed by the glory and political power of the kingdoms under David and Solomon. Under Solomon, Israel reached its highest point of prestige, wealth, and splendor, and much of the land which God promised Abraham temporarily came under the sway of Solomon.

Again, however, moral deterioration attacked from within. Because of Solomon's disregard of the law against marriage to the heathen, many of his wives were pagans who did not share his faith in God. His children, therefore, were raised by their pagan mothers and they were trained to worship idols instead of the God of Israel. The resulting judgment of God upon Israel was manifested in the divided kingdoms of Judah and Israel. The ten tribes, united to form the Kingdom of Israel, persisted in complete apostasy from God, and idol worship became the national religion. In 721 B.C. the ten tribes were carried off into captivity by the Assyrians. The Kingdom of Judah, including the tribes of Benjamin and Judah, continued for a little more than another century until they too were taken captive by Babylonia. For a generation, the land of Israel was denuded of the descendants of Abraham.

The book of Ezra records the restoration of Israel which followed the captivities. In keeping with the promise given to Jeremiah that the captivity would continue for only seventy years (Jeremiah 29:10), the first expedition of the children of Israel, led by Zerubbabel, began their trek to their homeland. The book of Ezra records their early steps in restoring the land and building the temple. Nehemiah completes the picture with the building of the walls and the restoration of the city of Jerusalem itself. Once again Israel was in their ancient land, re-established as a nation.

The history of Israel from that point on was not without its serious problems. First, the warriors of Macedon under Alexander the Great swept over Palestine. Then they were subject to the rule of the Seleucian monarchs and later were controlled by Syrians. One of the sad chapters in Israel's history was the Maccabean revolt which occurred in 167 B.C. and which resulted in severe persecution of the people of Israel. In 63 B.C. Pompey established Roman control and from then on the land of Palestine, the homeland of Israel, was under Roman control for centuries. It was in this period that Jesus Christ was born in Bethlehem. During Christ's lifetime on earth, Israel was under the heel of Rome and Christ Himself was sent to the cross on the basis of Roman authority.

THE HISTORY OF ISRAEL SINCE CHRIST

The subsequent history of Israel was most unhappy. In A.D. 70, Titus, the Roman general, ordered Jerusalem and its beautiful temple destroyed, and a quarter of a million Jews perished. The remaining Jews continued to revolt and finally in A.D. 135 the desolation of Judea was ordered. Almost a thousand towns and villages were left in ashes and fifty fortresses razed to the ground. The people of Israel, except for a few scattered families who remained, were dispersed to the four winds.

From A.D. 135 to modern times, the nation Israel made their homes all over the world. In the eighth century the Abbasid Arabs took possession of Israel's ancient land. For a brief period the Frankish crusaders were established in Palestine only to be defeated by Saladin in 1187. The Ottoman Turks assumed power in 1517 and the land of Palestine continued as part of the Ottoman Empire until Turkey was defeated in World War I. The conquering of Palestine by General Allenby in 1917 and the British occupation of Palestine proved to be a dramatic turning point in the history of Israel.

THE RETURN OF ISRAEL TO THE LAND

Before control of Palestine was wrested from the Turks, the Zionist movement had already begun. As early as 1871 some efforts were made by the Jews to re-establish themselves in a small way, but in the entire area there was not one Jewish village and only the more learned were familiar with the Hebrew tongue. In 1881 modern Zionist resettlement began in earnest. At that time only 25,000 Jews lived in the entire area. The Zionist idea as stated in "The Basle Programme" was adopted by the first Zionist congress called by Theodor Herzl in 1897. Its published aim was to reclaim the land of Palestine as the home for Jewish people. By the outbreak of World War I, the number of Jews had swelled to 80,000.

The Zionist movement was given impetus during World War I when British Foreign Secretary Arthur J. Balfour instituted the Balfour Declaration on November 2, 1917, in which he stated: "His Majesty's Government views with favor the establishment in Palestine of a national home for the Jewish people. . . ." This declaration, though welcomed by the Jews, was opposed by the Arabs and little came of it. Meanwhile a British mandate given over the land of Palestine by the League of Nations became effective, but through a desire of the British to maintain friendship with the Arab nations, no progress was allowed in establishing a homeland for Israel.

In 1939, during the early portion of World War II, the British government issued a white paper which set forth the conditions for establishing an independent Arab state in Palestine. By that time, 400,000 Jews were in the country. The restrictions on Jewish immigration, however, were severe, and future immigration was subject to Arab consent. Only a small part of the land could be sold to the Jews.

During World War II, however, due to the world-wide sympathy aroused for the people of Israel because of the slaughter of six million Jews under Nazi domination, the feeling became widespread that Israel should have a homeland to which its refugees could come and establish themselves. An Arab league was formed in 1945 to oppose further Jewish expansion. After World War II the British government turned Palestine over to the United Nations and under the direction of this body a partition of Palestine was recommended with the division into a Jewish state and an Arab state. By 1948 Jewish population had risen to 650,000.

THE ESTABLISHMENT OF THE NEW STATE OF ISRAEL

On May 14, 1948, as the British withdrew control, Israel proclaimed itself an independent state within the boundaries set up by the United Nations. Before the day passed, however, Israel was attacked by Egypt, Jordan, Iraq, Syria, Lebanon, and Saudi Arabia, and open warfare broke out. Though both sides suffered heavily, a series of truces began. The first was on June 11 and was followed by a renewal of hostilities which ended in a final truce on July 17. On January 7, 1949, a general armistice was arranged in which Israel was allowed to retain the additional land secured during the hostilities. Israel itself was admitted to the United Nations. In the years that followed no adequate solution was found for the many difficulties attending a permanent peace. The Arab nations refused to recognize Israel and denied it the right of existence. Israel on her part adopted an unrealistic approach to the refugee problem which continued to be an open sore.

Since 1949, the nation Israel has made rapid strides until today it is well established. Though surrounded by enemies, Israel rests in its security of superior arms and effective military organization. Of significance is the unassailable fact, that for the first time since A.D. 70, the nation Israel is independent and self-sustaining, and is recognized as a political state.

The restoration of Israel to its ancient land and its establishment as a political government is almost without parallel in the history of the world. Never before has an ancient people, scattered for so many centuries, been able to return to their ancient land and re-establish themselves with such success and such swift progress as is witnessed in the new state of Israel.

POLITICAL AND MILITARY GROWTH OF ISRAEL

Of special significance is the fact that Israel is a recognized political state. In its original declaration on May 14, 1948, provision was made for the establishment of an ordered government in the form of a democratic parliamentary republic. The principal legislative body in Israel is the knesset, from a Hebrew word which means "assembly." The knesset meets in Jerusalem, which is the capitol of Israel, and temporarily occupies quarters adapted for this purpose. A government center is planned on an elevation which will face Mount Herzl where the founder of the Zionist movement is buried. The knesset has power to make and amend laws, and its approval is necessary before a government can take office. A new government must be formed at such times as the knesset votes no confidence in the existing government. Of its 120 members, the great majority are of Jewish background, but a few Arabs are included.

The constitution of Israel provides that any citizen over twenty-one may be elected, and each citizen over eighteen, without respect to sex, race, or religion, is entitled to vote for members of the knesset. Though most matters of law are handled by civil courts divided into three main categories — namely, magistrate courts, district courts, and the supreme court — a series of special courts corresponding to the religion of respective citizens have been established in regard to marriage, divorce, and similar matters. A Jew therefore is referred to the rabbinical courts, Moslems to the Moslem court, and Christians to the Christian court. All of the religious courts are under the control of the Ministry of Religion. The internal government of Israel allows considerable freedom to minority groups, and provides a proper legal basis for this enterprising nation to grow.

One of the important factors of Israel's progress has

been its highly efficient army. Formed under great difficulty during the early days of the state of Israel when they were being attacked by enemies on all sides, through heroic efforts, it was able to give a good account of itself and actually enlarge the area of Israel by some fifty per cent in the resulting hostilities. The army is called in Hebrew *Tsahal*, representing the initials of the defense army in Israel known in Hebrew as the *Tseva Hagana Leisrael*. Included in its organization are forces equipped to fight on land, sea, and air. The army has been trained by experienced officers from Europe and America and several military academies and a staff college have been created.

The corps of the army consists of volunteers who are supplemented by reserves. Men on reaching the age of eighteen serve for two and one half years. They are eligible for service until they are forty-five. Single women are also given two years of training. A system has been devised by which reservists are settled in border areas and Israel is reputed to have the fastest mobilization system of any nation in the world. Along with the development of the army itself has been the creation of an arms industry which has enabled Israel not only to supply its own forces, but to export in large quantities arms of various kinds, including one of the best automatic weapons available today.

Humanly speaking, it is because of the efficiency of their army that Israel has enjoyed peace since the armistice of 1949 and was able to overrun the Gaza Strip in the hostilities which broke out in October, 1956. Though the nations which surround Israel number some thirty million and conceivably could overwhelm the small nation, the army of Israel is more than a match for all of its enemies combined. Because of this, the nation Israel today is in a high state of confidence coupled with alertness.

DEVELOPMENT OF AGRICULTURE AND INDUSTRY

Probably the most astounding aspect of the restoration of Israel is the rapid reclamation of the eroded land and wasted resources which for centuries have characterized the area which Israel now occupies. Travelers who visit Syria and Jordan first before coming to Israel are immediately impressed with the dramatic difference. Everywhere there is evidence of astounding progress in Israel.

One of the first problems which beset Israel was to reclaim the land strewn with rocks and seemingly hopeless as far as vegetation was concerned. By prodigious toil, often on the part of immigrants who had little knowledge of agriculture before, the land was cleared, terraced, and cultivated. In Israel, as in surrounding countries, the scarcity of water is a principal problem. Huge projects provided water for irrigation, not only for the northern portion of the nation, but also for the reclamation of the Negiv, the southern desert which forms a major portion of Israel's territory.

Travelers through Israel are introduced to field after field of cultivated crops on land that was hopelessly eroded just a few years before. By 1961, eighty million trees had been planted, and the continuing program eventually will make a major contribution in conserving water and providing timber. Orange trees have been planted in abundance, as well as other citrus fruits, and oranges have become a major export of the new nation. Crops such as cotton, sugar cane, grapes, peanuts, and sisal have become major productions. Just a few years ago eggs were closely rationed. By 1961 Israel was exporting almost a million eggs a day.

Though hampered somewhat by failure to conclude peace agreements with Arab nations which share the water available, by making the most of its own opportunities, Israel is building a gigantic irrigation system, drawing water from the Yarkon as well as from the Jordan and sending it south to the Negiv. Thousands of acres are being restored to fertility, and it is estimated that the reclaimed land will permit another one million immigrants during the next decade. Not only have desert lands been reclaimed, but one of the spectacular achievements was the draining of the swampland of the Valley of Esdraelon, the elimination of the mosquito menace, and the restoration of this broad area to cultivation, which has proved to be one of the most fertile areas in all Israel.

Progress in agriculture and reclamation of the land has been matched to some extent by establishment of industries. Textiles have now become an important part of Israel's production. The cutting of diamonds imported for this purpose, the manufacture of military weapons and arms, and the exploitation of the measureless chemical wealth of the Dead Sea are major factors of Israel's economy. Some oil has already been discovered as well as gas. One by one problems that beset Israel at the beginning are being solved.

The expanding economy has also furnished a basis for construction of fabulous new cities. The new city of Jerusalem, the capitol of Israel, has been beautifully constructed of stone with lovely streets and parks and by 1961 had attained a population of 160,000. Tel Aviv, the largest of the cities in Israel, has a population nearing 400,000, and offers every convenience of a modern city. Next to Tel Aviv is Haifa, with a population of 175,000. The growth of the cities has kept up with the growth in population which has almost tripled since 1948, reaching over two million in 1960.

EDUCATIONAL SYSTEM AND REVIVAL OF BIBLICAL HEBREW

One of the impressive sights in Israel is the spectacular rise of its educational system. Not only are new elementary schools built throughout the country to take care of the expanding population, but the Hebrew university with an enrollment in 1959-60 of seven thousand is one of the finest in the Middle East. In addition the Israel Institute of Technology has some twenty-five hundred students with training in various aspects of modern science. In the entire educational system Biblical Hebrew is used as the spoken and written language and has restored this ancient language to popular usage in Israel. New terms are being coined to meet modern situations. The revival of Hebrew inevitably ties the people of Israel to their ancient Scriptures in a way that otherwise would have been impossible.

The revival of Hebrew has also paved the way for a renewal of Biblical studies. Unlike American universities which neglect the Bible, the Old Testament is taught in public schools, including the universities, and is considered essential to any true education. Some four hundred study groups have been formed by the Israel Bible Study Association with a membership approaching twenty thousand. The reading of the Old Testament is popular, though often attended by little theological discernment. Even the New Testament is read as religious literature, though not considered on a par with the Old Testament by orthodox Jews. To some extent the new interest in the Bible has created an increased interest in the Jewish religion as such.

RELIGIOUS LIFE OF ISRAEL

It is to be expected with the rebirth of the nation and its renewed interest in the Bible that attendance at the synagogue has taken on new life in Israel. Visitors normally will find the synagogue crowded, though meeting in new and spacious buildings. It soon becomes evident, however, that the religious life of Israel is to some extent one of outer form. The religious exercises are devoted primarily to revival of their traditions, their reassurance of the general providence of God, and the application to some extent of moral standards. For Israel their religion is one of works rather than of faith, and their redemption is to be achieved by their own efforts.

The religious life of Israel is directed by some 430 rabbis who actively carry on their duties. It is to these leaders that Israel turns for direction. As a result of the revival of Judaism, the Sabbath is strictly enforced and everyone observes it, even those who never attend the synagogue. The religious life of Israel is largely in the hands of the orthodox, though the majority of ordinary Jews in Israel do not necessarily follow their leaders. The revival of interest, therefore, in the Jewish faith and the religious activities which characterize it, to some extent is an expression of patriotism and enthusiasm for the progress of the state rather than for theological or spiritual reasons. Nevertheless, the movement is a phenomenon without parallel in the modern history of Israel and is doing much to revive their ancient faith. The land of Israel which historically has been the cradle of Judaism, Christianity, and the Moslem faith is once again witnessing a revival of that which held sway for centuries.

POLITICAL AND PROPHETIC SIGNIFICANCE OF THE NEW STATE OF ISRAEL

The significance of the new state of Israel is bound up with the growing importance of the Middle East in international affairs. The land of Israel is located geographically in the hub of three major continents. Because of this strategic location, it is involved in the economic life of the world. Any major nation seeking to dominate the world would need to conquer this portion. Its military value is also obvious, for the Middle East is not only a channel of world commerce but is the gateway to the immense reserves in oil and chemicals found in that portion of the world. It is inevitable that any future world conflict would engulf this portion of the world as a primary objective. It is especially significant that from a Biblical standpoint the Middle East remains a center of interest. World events which are yet to unfold will find this area also its major theater. It is for this reason that students of the Bible, whether Jews or Christians, find the development of the new state of Israel one of the most important and significant events of the twentieth century.

The repossession of a portion of their ancient land by the new state of Israel is especially striking because of the promise given by God to Abraham of perpetual title to the land between Egypt and the Euphrates. As recorded in Genesis 15:18 the covenant of God with Abraham included the promise: "Unto thy seed have I given this land, from the river of Egypt unto the great river, the river Euphrates." This promise was subsequently repeated in Genesis 17:8

in these words: "And I will give unto thee, and to thy seed after thee, the land of thy sojournings, all the land of Canaan, for an everlasting possession; and I will be their God." Consideration will be given to these passages in later discussion, but their mention at this time demonstrates the great significance of the reoccupation of this area by the new state of Israel.

In the subsequent history of Israel neither Abraham nor his immediate posterity were able to possess the land and, as stated earlier, only at the time of the Exodus was the land ever actually possessed. Of great importance are the Scriptures which describe the dispersion of Israel in the captivities of Babylon and Assyria and the later scattering of Israel resulting from the persecution of the Romans. This will be followed by Israel's ultimate regathering. A study of some of the great promises relating to this future restoration of Israel to the land will be examined in detail later. The revival of Israel after these many centuries of dispersion introduces the major questions relating to the fulfillment of God's promise to Abraham and whether the creation of the new state of Israel is indeed a confirmation of Israel's continuance as a nation.

The return of Israel and the organization of the new state of Israel is especially significant in the light of prophecies to be examined concerning Israel's future time of trouble when Israel is pictured in the land, as for instance in Matthew 24:15-26. The predictions of the grand climax of the nation's history, given in Daniel 9:26, 27, when Israel is described as making a covenant with the future world ruler, is of special importance in the light of their renewed presence in their ancient land. Of the many peculiar phenomena which characterize the present generation, few events can claim equal significance as far as Biblical prophecy is concerned with that of the return of Israel to their land. It constitutes a preparation for the end of the age, the setting for the coming of the Lord for His church, and the fulfillment of Israel's prophetic destiny.

Chapter II

THE PROMISE TO ABRAHAM

In approaching the study of eschatology, the theology of Biblical prophecy, one is plunged immediately into a major division of divine revelation which is determinative in theology as a whole. Eschatology is the doctrine of last things, the word being derived from *eschatos*, meaning *last*, and *logos*, referring to theology as a rational science. In its larger dimension, it includes all that was prophetically future at the time it was revealed. This is subject to further subdivision into eschatology which has been fulfilled and eschatology which is still future or unfulfilled.

In modern theology this simple definition has become obscured. The modern concept of "realized" eschatology reduces its status to that of divine purpose. By so doing, it robs eschatology of its quality of specific prediction of the future. This point of view is based on the idea that it is impossible for anyone, even for writers of the Word of God, to predict the future.

Orthodox theology, however, has never submitted to such a limitation and throughout the history of the church it has been assumed that the Bible can speak authoritatively on things to come. Though there is evident difference of opinion as to how prophecy should be interpreted, the orthodox position does not question the authenticity of prophecy itself. In this discussion, it is assumed that the Bible in its original writings was given by inspiration of God and is an infallible revelation of His mind and purpose. The problem before us then is not one of demonstrating the validity of prophecy or the accuracy of the Scriptures. It is rather one of theological induction and interpretation of the revelation given in the Bible.

MAJOR DIVISIONS OF THE DIVINE PROGRAM

In order to approach the subject of eschatology intelligently, some principle of organization must be adopted in the interpretation of the broad and extensive field of Scriptural prophecy. Among a number of possibilities, two such principles may be mentioned by way of introduction.

First, the eschatological program of God may be considered in four major divisions: (1) The program for angels, including the present ministry and future blessedness of the elect angels and the present activity and future damnation of fallen angels, usually embraced in the branch of systematic theology called satanology. (2) The program of God for Gentiles embodied in the broad provisions of God's covenant with Adam and Noah and subsequently unfolded in the visions given to the Prophet Daniel in the book that bears his name. Included in God's program for the Gentiles is provision for the salvation of those who turn to God in true faith. (3) The divine program for Israel is unfolded in the Abrahamic, Palestinian, Davidic and new covenants and in a large measure is unfolded as the principal subject of the Old Testament beginning in Genesis 12. It includes all of God's dealings with Israel in the past and predicts a consummation in the future, when a time of great tribulation will befall the nation. The time of tribulation will be followed by Israel's regathering, restoration, and glory in the millennial kingdom. It is this division which will constitute our area of study. (4) The divine program for the church unfolded in the New Testament consisting in the divine program in the present age and its eschatological consummation in the translation of the church, its judgment, and reward. As presented in the New Testament, it falls into two broad areas: (a) the professing church, i.e. Christendom, destined to become a world religion of apostate character before its ultimate judgment by God at the second coming of Christ; (b) the calling out of the true church, the body of Christ, within the professing church, composed of Jew and Gentile alike on equal basis joined by the baptism of the Spirit, placed in Christ, born again of the

Spirit of God, and indwelt by the triune God. The salvation and sanctification of those who form the body of Christ
is the central purpose of God in this present age and in
some sense suspends the progress of God's dealings with
the Gentile nations and Israel until God's purpose for the
church has been realized.

ALTERNATE APPROACH OF COVENANT THEOLOGY

The fourfold division suggested for the program of
God for His moral creatures is a comprehensive and illumi-
nating approach to the tremendous mass of Scriptures which
bear upon the divine purpose of God. An alternative to
this is provided by a second approach, that of the so-called
covenant theologians. It is not our purpose to deal in detail with this point of view, but its principal elements can
be stated. It is the assumption of the covenant theologian
that the major purpose of God is the salvation of the elect,
embodied in a covenant of grace or covenant of redemption,
and that all other purposes of God are subordinate to this.
For this reason the divine revelation as it relates to angels
is usually ignored as somewhat irrelevant. The contrast
between God's program for Israel and the church is usually replaced by the concept that the church is a continuation
of true Israel or that the church embraces all the saved
of all ages.

At least two major objections can be mentioned op-
posing the covenant theologians' interpretation. First, the
covenant theologian is guilty of the reductive error, namely,
taking one facet of God's divine program and making it
all-determinative. It leaves without adequate explanation
the dealings of God with the natural world, and with the
mass of unsaved humanity, which is regarded simply as
an unfortunate context for God's major purpose. Second,
the interpretation of Scripture required for covenant theology involves passing over the specifics of hundreds of
prophecies in Scripture and taking these either in a spiritualized sense or ignoring them altogether.

Preferable is the point of view that regards God's

major purpose in the universe as that of self-manifestation. In this approach the *summum bonum* is the manifestation of the infinite perfections of God which constitute His glory. With this point of view, the natural world takes on wonderful meaning in that "the heavens declare the glory of God." The salvation of the elect in all dispensations is recognized as a major aspect of manifesting His glory, for in this alone can His infinite love and righteousness merge in grace, but other aspects of the divine program are not displaced. The separate programs of God for the angels, Gentiles, Israel, and the church each bring out different facets of God's infinite perfection such as righteousness in relation to the angels, faithfulness in relation to Israel, sovereignty in relation to the Gentiles, and grace and truth in relation to the church. Even the condemnation of the lost, pre-eminently demonstrating God's infinite righteousness and holiness, is seen in the context of divine love in that their hopeless estate was needless because Christ has died for them.

PRINCIPLE OF INTERPRETATION

In the broad approach of interpretation of prophecy attention needs to be given to two alternative principles of interpretation. That adopted in this study is the principle that Scripture should be interpreted in its normative, literal sense, except in such instances where a figurative or nonliteral interpretation is obviously indicated. In applying this principle no distinction needs to be observed between Scripture which is noneschatological and Scripture which is eschatological. The same hermeneutical principles which apply to any other portion of Scripture apply equally well to eschatology.

An alternative point of view was advanced by Augustine who suggested a dual hermeneutics, namely, that while all Scripture should be interpreted normally — that is, literally — prophecy or eschatology was to be understood in a figurative or nonliteral way. His principal reason for this dual hermeneutics was that a literal interpretation of prophecy would lead to chiliasm, or the premillennial interpretation.

Modern amillenarians have not improved much on Augustine's original dismissal of premillennialism. Their principal objection continues to be that the premillennial system is hopelessly confused and self-contradictory. The answer to this objection, while having many facets, is in the main a demonstration that premillennial interpretation is not only consistent with Scripture but consistent with itself and provides a program for eschatology which is not afforded in any other point of view.

It will be impossible within the confines of this study to debate in any satisfactory way the question of premillennialism versus amillennialism. This has been presented many times by competent scholars. Such works as J. Dwight Pentecost's *Things to Come;* Charles Feinberg's *Premillennialism or Amillennialism?;* Alva J. McClain's *The Greatness of the Kingdom;* Lewis Sperry Chafer's *Systematic Theology; The Basis of the Premillennial Faith* by Charles Ryrie; and my own volume, *The Millennial Kingdom,* set forth a sufficient answer for those who are willing to examine their pages.

The purpose of this study will be to examine Biblical prophecies relating to Israel and the theological implications arising from such an interpretation. The approach would be basically Scriptural and the reasonableness of the interpretation its own major defense. The best answer to the charge that there is no distinction between Israel and the church and similar amillennial dictums is to present what the Scriptures actually reveal. Fundamental to this whole point of view is the exegesis and interpretation of the Abrahamic covenant.

EXEGESIS OF THE ABRAHAMIC COVENANT

The first statement of the covenant of God made with Abraham, given in Genesis 12:1-3, was originally delivered to Abraham while still in Ur of the Chaldees and is stated in these words: "Get thee out of thy country, and from thy kindred, and from thy father's house, unto the land that I will show thee: and I will make of thee a great nation, and

I will bless thee, and make thy name great; and be thou a blessing: and I will bless them that bless thee, and him that curseth thee will I curse: and in thee shall all the families of the earth be blessed." God promised Abraham that subject to his obedience to the command to leave his own country and go to a land that God would show him, certain blessings would accrue to him.

First, certain promises were given to Abraham personally. Of Abraham, God would make a great nation. His divine blessing would rest upon Abraham. His name would be great. Abraham himself would be a blessing. In regard to Abraham, God promised a special circumstance in which He would bless those who blessed Abraham and would curse those who cursed him. The blessing promised through Abraham, according to verse three, was to extend to all families of the earth.

Second, though the Abrahamic covenant as given was directed primarily to Abraham as a person, it is obvious that out of it come two other major aspects of the covenant. Not only did God direct promises to Abraham himself, but the promise was given of the formation of a great nation out of Abraham. Third, the blessings falling on Abraham and his descendants would reach out unto all other families of the earth. Hence, an ordinary exegesis of the Abrahamic covenant in its original pronouncement involves (1) promises to Abraham; (2) promises to the nation, i.e., Israel; (3) promise of blessing to all nations, i.e., the Gentiles.

The prophecy of this Scripture is enriched by further revelation given later. In Genesis 12:7 God declared to Abraham: "Unto thy seed will I give this land." The promise of the land is reiterated in Genesis 13:14-17 where Abraham is exhorted to survey the land in all directions. In addition, Abraham's seed, destined to occupy the land, is described as being as numerous as the dust of the earth.

The dimensions of the land promised to the seed of Abraham are recorded in Genesis 15:18-20. The entire area from the river of Egypt unto the Euphrates river is

given to Abraham and his posterity as a perpetual possession. Further details are given concerning the promise to
Abraham in Genesis 17:1-8, including the fact that he would
have a multitude of seed, and would be the father of many
nations. In recognition of this his name is changed from
Abram, meaning "exalted father," to Abraham, meaning
"father of a multitude." It is further promised that he
would be exceedingly fruitful (17:6) and that kings would
descend from him. The covenant with Abraham is declared in verse seven to be everlasting and the promise of
possession of the land forever is reiterated in verse eight.
The Abrahamic covenant is subject to further elucidation
in Genesis 22:15-18 after Abraham's seed is limited to
Abraham's son Isaac in Genesis 21:12, in the words: "For
in Isaac shall thy seed be called." Taking into consideration
the fact that Isaac had two sons, Jacob and Esau, the promise
is further limited to Jacob and his descendants in Genesis
28:13, 14 in the revelation: "I am Jehovah, the God of
Abraham thy father, and the God of Isaac: the land whereon
thou liest, to thee will I give it, and to thy seed: and thy
seed shall be as the dust of the earth, and thou shalt
spread abroad to the west, and to the east, and to the north,
and to the south: and in thee, and in thy seed shall all the
families of the earth be blessed."

These many Scriptures dealing with the Abrahamic
covenant will be discussed more at length later, but their
mere itemization establishes the basic promises embodied in
the Abrahamic covenant which can now be summarized
as follows: (1) Abraham's name shall be great. (2) Abraham
shall personally have great blessing. (3) Whoever will
bless Abraham will be blessed and whoever will curse
Abraham will be cursed. (4) From Abraham will come a
great nation, innumerable as the dust of the earth. (5)
Abraham will be the father of many nations, not just one.
(6) Kings shall come from the line of Abraham. (7) Abraham's seed shall inherit the land from the river of Egypt to
the Euphrates river as an everlasting possession. (8) God
will be the God of Abraham and his seed forever. (9) Abra-

ham's seed shall conquer their enemies. (10) In Abraham's seed all the nations of the earth shall be blessed. (11) The covenant with Abraham shall be an everlasting covenant. (12) The promises to Abraham's seed are narrowed to the descendants of Isaac. (13) The promises to Abraham's seed are narrowed to descendants of Jacob, especially as pertaining to the land and the promise of blessing to all nations.

In arriving at these details, the plain language of Scripture and the promises of the Abrahamic covenant have simply been itemized. If the facts stand as they seem to be presented in the Scriptures, a massive presentation of the divine purpose of God for Abraham's seed is thus unfolded. It is a dramatic declaration of a new divine purpose quite different from His declared purpose for Gentiles as a whole. A particular rill of humanity has been sovereignly chosen to fulfill a divine purpose distinct in its character and in its fulfillment.

It is obvious, however, to any interpreter of Scripture that all will not agree on such a literal interpretation of these promises and it is therefore necessary to give attention not only to the exegesis but to the interpretation of the words and statements embodied in the Abrahamic covenant and its subsequent enlargement and repetition. Two major considerations confront the interpreter of the Abrahamic covenant: (1) Are these promises to be taken simply and literally, or are they to be interpreted in a nonliteral or figurative sense? (2) Are the promises embodied in the Abrahamic covenant sovereignly given or are they contingent upon subsequent obedience on the part of Abraham and his seed? In brief, the issue is literal versus spiritualized interpretation, and the question of whether the covenant is conditional or unconditional.

ARE THE PROMISES TO ABRAHAM LITERAL?

In approaching the interpretation of the Abrahamic covenant, one is faced with a determinative decision which goes far beyond the borders of specific promises of this covenant. The issue in a word is whether prophecy can be interpreted literally and normally or whether it should be understood in a figurative or spiritualized sense. The amillennial point of view requires extensive spiritualization of prophecy, whereas the premillennial interpretation is more literal. As related to the Abrahamic covenant, the question hinges on the interpretation of the expression, "the seed of Abraham," and the specifics that are promised. The problem has been somewhat confused by the fact that some premillenarians have tended to build their system upon an amillennial foundation and have not kept clearly in mind a proper basis for premillennial truth. In general, however, the premillennial point of view requires that the promises given to Abraham should be fulfilled by Abraham. Promises to Abraham's seed shall be fulfilled by his physical descendants, and promises made to "all families of the earth" will be fulfilled by Gentiles, i.e., those who are not physical descendants of Abraham. Hence, extreme care should be taken in determining precisely what promises are given to what peoples.

Guided by this principle, one can observe certain promises true only of Abraham, i.e., God's personal blessing upon him, the promise that his name shall be great, and that God will make a great nation of him. The promise given to all nations is limited to the idea that they shall be blessed through Abraham. This of course is subsequently enlarged in God's total program in grace for believing Gentiles in general and the church in particular. The crux of the interpretative problem, however, lies in the definition of the expression, "the seed of Abraham." How shall this expression be understood?

An examination of all references to the seed of Abraham in Scripture reveals that the expression is used in three distinct senses. First, there is the natural use, i.e., the natural seed of Abraham referring to those who are actual physical descendants of Abraham. Though there is a sense in which all natural descendants of Abraham are included, such as Ishmael and his descendants and Isaac and his descendants through Esau, it is clear that the particular promises of God to the seed are narrowed first to Isaac and then to Jacob and through Jacob to the twelve tribes of Israel. To them God promises in a special sense to be their God. To them was given the law of Moses, and the perpetual title to the Promised Land is given to them.

Second, the expression "the seed of Abraham" is used in special reference to the spiritual lineage coming from Abraham, that is, those in Israel who trusted in God, who kept the law, and qualified for many of the blessings of the covenant. It is evident, for instance, that all Israelites do not actually inherit the land and that only spiritual Israel will enter the future millennial kingdom and fulfill the promise. The distinction between natural Israel and spiritual Israel is revealed in such major passages as Romans 9-11 and specifically in Romans 9:6-8: "For they are not all Israel, that are of Israel: neither because they are Abraham's seed are they all children: but, in Isaac shall thy seed be called. That is, it is not the children of the flesh that are children of God; but the children of the promise are reckoned for a seed." It is evident then that the more particular promises of the Abrahamic covenant will not be fulfilled by all the natural seed, but by those in natural Israel who also qualify as spiritual seed. Further, the provision of divine sovereignty is that God apart from human merit determines the selection of Jacob instead of Esau (Romans 9:12, 13). In order to qualify, therefore, for the full promise of God to Israel, an individual had to be, first, of the natural seed of Abraham, i.e., a descendant of Jacob, and, second, one who trusted in God, thereby qualifying as belonging to the spiritual seed.

A third division, however, relating to the spiritual seed of Abraham is unfolded in Galatians 3:6-9 which reads as follows: "Even as Abraham believed God, and it was reckoned unto him for righteousness. Know therefore that they that are of faith, the same are sons of Abraham. And the scripture, foreseeing that God would justify the Gentiles by faith, preached the gospel beforehand unto Abraham, saying, In thee shall all the nations be blessed. So then they that are of faith are blessed with the faithful Abraham." Here we learn that there is also a spiritual seed of Abraham who are Gentiles, those who are not physical descendants of Abraham. Some, on the basis of this Galatians passage, have drawn the unwarranted conclusion that all distinctions between the natural seed of Abraham and the spiritual seed are thereby erased.

The passage itself, however, makes very clear that Gentiles who are recognized as the children of Abraham come under the promise given to the Gentiles and not under promises given to the physical seed of Abraham. The portion of the Abrahamic covenant which is quoted by Paul refers to the Gentiles in the words: "In thee shall all the nations be blessed." Paul's conclusion therefore is: "So then they that are of faith are blessed with the faithful Abraham." This means that they come under the blessing promised the nations, but it does not mean that they come under all the promises given to Abraham personally or to his seed in the physical sense. A Gentile in the present age is Abraham's seed because he is "in Christ Jesus" (Galatians 3:28). It is on this basis that Galatians 3:29 states: "And if you are Christ's, then are ye Abraham's seed, heirs according to promise."

A Gentile Christian therefore becomes the seed of Abraham not because of any physical lineage with Abraham himself nor simply by imitation of Abraham's faith, but because he is regarded by God as in Christ who is indeed a physical descendant of Abraham. The promises thereby assured are the promises given to Gentiles, not the particular promises given to Israel.

It may be concluded, therefore, that the seed of Abraham is used (1) of the natural seed of Abraham, more specifically the descendants of Jacob; (2) spiritual Israel, i.e., descendants of Jacob who trust in God; (3) Gentiles who are in Christ and are spiritual seed of Abraham, thereby qualifying for the promise of blessing to Gentiles in Abraham. Promises addressed to Abraham, therefore, can be apportioned according to the qualifying characteristic of each group. The promise given to Abraham that God would bless those who bless him, and curse those who curse him, has to some extent been extended to the entire nation of Israel, even to those who do not qualify as spiritual seed. History has demonstrated God's faithfulness in dealing with those who have oppressed His ancient people.

The realization of most of the promises, however, depends upon an individual Israelite being spiritual. Only thus will he ever enter into the future millennial kingdom, either as a survivor of the tribulation or as a resurrected saint. The blessings of God to Israel in this life as recorded in the Old Testament have been largely limited to spiritual Israel. Upon natural Israel in unbelief God has heaped His judgment and divine discipline. The promise to the spiritual seed of Abraham among the Gentiles is having a supreme demonstration in this present age in the calling out of the church composed largely of those who in their natural estate were Gentiles. The threefold distinction, therefore, in the seed of Abraham provides a solid basis for understanding eschatology as a whole while maintaining the proper distinction between Israel and the church and between Abraham's physical seed and Gentiles.

The principal opposition to this threefold distinction in the usage of the term "the seed of Abraham" arises from the amillennial interpretation and more particularly from those who embrace covenant theology. Illustrative of this amillennial point of view is the work, *The Seed of Abraham*, by Albertus Pieters. To him the term "the seed of Abraham" means only the spiritual seed of Abraham without distinction between Israel and Gentiles or between natural and spiritual. Pieters summarizes his point of view in these words: "The expression 'Seed of Abraham,' in biblical usage, denotes that visible community, the members of which stand in relation to God through the Abrahamic Covenant, and thus are heirs to the Abrahamic promise" (p. 20). He states further: "Whenever we meet with the argument that God made certain promises to the Jewish race, the above facts are pertinent. God never made any promises to any race at all, as a race. All His promises were to the continuing covenanted community, without regard to its racial constituents or to the personal ancestry of the individuals in it" (pp. 19, 20). He holds further that not only are the promises given only to the spiritual seed, but that the modern Jew of today has lost his lineage and there is no one qualified to inherit any promises given to the Jews as a race.

While it is not the intent here to provide a complete refutation of the amillennial exegesis of the Abrahamic covenant, certain important objections can be raised. First, the argument of Pieters rests on the assumption that there is no one today who is a physical descendant of Abraham. This extreme position is not shared by most amillenarians as it is faced by almost insuperable problems. The racial continuity of Israel, though marred by intermarriage with heathen, is recognized throughout the Scriptures. As late as the epistle of James, the twelve tribes are addressed (James 1:1). The Jews have been recognized by the world as a continuing people as manifested in the Zionist movement, the existence of the state of Israel today, the perpetuation of Israel's religion, and by almost universal recognition that the people of Israel are a distinct race. If the testimony of the book of Revelation may be introduced as evidence, one finds here again the twelve tribes of Israel specified by name as participating in the future great tribulation.

A notable weakness in the amillennial exegesis of the Abrahamic covenant is the fact that it does not take into consideration the specifics of God's revelation. Pieters for instance passes over Genesis 15:18-21 without even a word of comment, and the revelation that the covenant is everlasting and that the land is promised as an everlasting possession in Genesis 17:7, 8 is likewise given silent treatment. The fact is that any reasonable understanding of the terminology of these passages leads unmistakably to the conclusion that Abraham understood the promises as given to his physical seed, which forms the background of his special interest in Isaac and the promise of the land which evidently Abraham understood in a physical way. It is true that Abraham's faith went beyond the promise of the physical land to that of the heavenly city, the New Jerusalem in the eternal state, as indicated in Hebrews 11:10. But the promise of the land is obviously related to the temporal and will be fulfilled as long as the present earth lasts, whereas the promise of the eternal city had to do with the eternal state.

A spiritualized understanding of the promises of the land becomes ridiculous in that the land has to be made to mean heaven. The description given of the land in Genesis 15:15-18 as extending from the river of Egypt to the river Euphrates and including godless and pagan tribes is hardly a suitable terminology for the description of heaven. The efforts to understand the Abrahamic covenant in a specialized interpretation ultimately destroys any exegesis of these passages and changes the intended revelation to the point where the words used no longer have proper meaning. Premillenarians agree that there is a spiritual seed of Abraham, and that these inherit the appropriate promises addressed to spiritual Israel or spiritual Gentiles as the case may be. They deny that this requires spiritualization of the promises as pertaining to the physical seed of Abraham and the promises relating to the land. Further attention will be given these features later.

ARE THE PROMISES TO ABRAHAM CONDITIONAL?

The traditional amillennial interpretation of the Abrahamic promises tends to follow the method of spiritualizing them, thereby removing the element of specific and literal predictions. Another device, however, adopted by modern amillenarians, follows the argument that the promises are conditional. Under this approach a literal interpretation of the promise can be followed, i.e., it may be held that Israel was actually promised the land and other blessings, but it is charged that Israel failed to meet the conditions.

Therefore the promises are withdrawn. Such is the approach of Oswald Allis in his book, *Prophecy and the Church.*

Allis states his support of the conditional element in the Abrahamic covenant in these words: "It is true that, in the express terms of the covenant with Abraham, obedience is not stated as a condition. But that obedience was presupposed is clearly indicated by two facts. The one is that obedience is the precondition of blessing under all circumstances. . . . The second fact is that in the case of Abraham the duty of obedience is particularly stressed" (p. 33).

It is true that, in some cases in the Bible, promises are given in a conditional way. For instance, the Mosaic covenant contains many conditional promises, i.e., blessing for obedience, cursing or divine judgment for disobedience. However, it is not true that in Scripture obedience is always the condition of blessing. Allis, who is a Calvinist, has forgotten his doctrine of unconditional election. He has also forgotten the principle of divine grace in which God blesses those who are unworthy. The fact is that many of God's blessings fall upon those who are the least worthy of them. In such a doctrine as the security of the believer, which Allis would be the first to support, there is recognition of the principle that God makes promises which depend on Himself and His grace, not on human faithfulness. It certainly is not true that God's promises or that prophecy as a whole is conditioned upon human action. The major premise of Allis therefore, that obedience is always the condition of blessing, is a fallacy. God is able to make promises and keep them regardless of what men may do.

The second aspect of the position of Allis, that in the case of Abraham the duty of obedience is particularly stressed, is true in itself, but it does not affect the argument. In several instances in Abraham's life he was disobedient and in none of these instances did God withdraw the promise of the covenant. On other occasions when Abraham was obedient God reiterated the promise and added further details. But never was the promise made contingent upon later obedience. As a matter of fact, the history of Israel abounds in records of their disobedience, and yet the covenant of God given through Abraham is repeated in various ways and confirmed throughout the entire Old Testament.

There is, however, a partial validity to the point of view of Allis, namely, that under the covenant an individual Israelite would qualify for personal blessings by obedience which he would not receive if he were disobedient. For instance, when Israel was obedient they were blessed in the land. When they were disobedient they were removed and taken away into captivity. The ultimate fulfillment of the covenant with Abraham, however, was never in jeopardy as even in the midst of their apostasy they were given strongest assurances of being brought back into the land in subsequent generations and of their continuance as a nation.

Amillenarians are wont to bring up numerous problems, such as the conditional judgment pronounced upon Ninevah by Jonah, the judgment upon Eli's house, and limitation and application of blessings of the Abrahamic covenant to the spiritual scene. These have been answered in detail by premillenarians (cf. *The Millennial Kingdom* by the writer, pp. 154 ff). In a word, conditional promises under the Mosaic covenant do not affect the Abrahamic covenant. There is a proper answer to every amillennial objection, and the support of the concept that the Abrahamic covenant is unconditional is abundant.

The evidence that the covenant with Abraham is unconditional should be understood as supporting the idea that the complete fulfillment of the covenant was rendered sure when God gave it to Abraham in the first place. By using the word unconditional, it is not intended to imply that there were no human contingencies, but rather that God took all these contingencies into consideration when He made the promise. Further, it should be understood that the promise is not necessarily in all of its aspects fulfilled to every individual Israelite, but that some aspects of the promise are reserved for particular Israelites in a particular generation and limited to a large extent to those in Israel who are qualified as the spiritual seed of Abraham. The promise is not necessarily fulfilled therefore by *all* the seed of Abraham, but by *some* of the seed of Abraham.

The unconditional aspect of the Abrahamic covenant is confirmed by the fact that all of Israel's covenants are unconditional except the Mosaic. In the statement of the covenant itself no conditions are itemized. When confirmations are given, while these sometimes arise from some act of obedience or devotion, it is not implied thereby that the covenant itself is conditioned. Further, the covenant with Abraham was confirmed by the unqualified oath of God symbolized in the shedding of blood and passing between parts of the sacrifice as described in Genesis 15:7-21. While circumcision was required to recognize an individual as being within the covenant, it is not made the *sine qua non* of the fulfillment of the covenant. In fact, the Abrahamic covenant was given before the rite of circumcision was introduced. Not only was the covenant confirmed without conditions to Isaac and Jacob, but later it was reiterated to the people of Israel in times of disobedience and apostasy, the most notable case being that of Jeremiah, when the nation was promised that it would continue forever (Jeremiah 31:36). The New Testament declares the Abrahamic covenant immutable (Hebrews 6:13-18). A study of later covenants tends to support the unconditional character of the Abrahamic. The idea therefore that the Abrahamic covenant is suspended and inoperative because of sin in the lives of descendants of Abraham is untenable. If a literal interpretation of the promises is allowed, literal fulfillment can be expected.

SUMMARY

The prophetic program of God for Israel is therefore one of the four major programs revealed in the Bible: (1) The program of God for angels. (2) The program of God for Gentiles. (3) The program of God for the church.

(4) The program of God for Israel. This approach is far superior to that of the covenant theologians as it comprehends all events of all classifications and relates them to the total divine program in which God manifests His own infinite perfections to His own glory. It further permits a normal and literal interpretation of prophecy in the same way as is used in interpreting other forms of Scriptural revelation.

The Abrahamic covenant contributes to the eschatology of Israel by detailing the broad program of God as it affects Abraham's seed. It includes promises to Abraham personally, promises to the nation as such, and promises of blessing through Israel to the Gentiles. Important in the Abrahamic covenant is the promise as directed to the seed which is limited in subsequent Scripture to Isaac, and then Jacob, and then the twelve sons of Jacob. The question of whether the promises to Abraham should be interpreted literally was shown to hinge on the question of literal interpretation of the expression "the seed of Abraham." It was shown that this expression has a threefold use in the Bible — first, to the natural seed of Abraham, that is, all of his physical descendants; second, to the seed of Abraham who followed Abraham's noble example of faith, i.e., the Israel who trusted in God; and, third, the spiritual seed of Abraham, that is, Gentiles who qualify for the promise given to the nations. Evidence was adduced that the promises given to Abraham's physical seed will be fulfilled in his literal descendants who qualify spiritually, whereas promises given to the spiritual seed who are not physical descendants of Abraham inherit the promises given to Gentiles. This approach allowed a normal and literal interpretation of the Abrahamic covenant. The second leading question, namely, are the promises given to Abraham conditional? was answered by pointing to Scriptures that affirm the unalterable purpose of God that Israel should be a nation forever and should possess the land forever. Amillennial arguments to the contrary were considered and found without adequate basis. It is not too much to say that the exegesis of the

Abrahamic covenant and its resulting interpretation is the foundation for the study of prophecy as a whole, not only as relating to Israel, but also for the Gentiles and the church. It is here that the true basis for a premillennial interpretation of the Scriptures is found.

CHAPTER III

ISRAEL'S FUTURE AS A NATION

One of the central questions in prophecy relating to Israel is whether Israel has any future as a nation. The question is by no means easily answered because there is a confusing number of answers to the question. These can be itemized as follows: (1) The point of view that denies that Israel exists today and therefore has no future as a nation, as illustrated in the book *The Seed of Abraham* by Albertus Pieters. In Pieters' opinion, Israel is nonexistent as either a race or a nation in the ordinary sense of the term. (2) The idea that Israel continues as a race but not as a nation. This concept is illustrated in conservative postmillennialism of the last generation in works like *Systematic Theology* by Charles Hodge and is held by some contemporary amillenarians such as William Hendriksen in his book *And So All Israel Shall Be Saved*. (3) The teaching of most premillenarians that Israel has not only continuity as a race, but a future as a nation in the millennial kingdom. This is the normal premillennial approach.

Variations in the statement of these three major points of view abound. The opinion of Albertus Pieters has already been discussed and the evident facts pointing to the continuance of Israel as a race have been stated. The formation of a political state in the Middle East in 1948 bearing the name Israel as well as the continuance of Judaism as a religion seems a sufficient answer to the first point of view. The principal question which remains is whether Israel continues merely as a race without a future or whether it has promises which can be fulfilled only by its continuance as a nation and its revival as a people in the political government of the millennial kingdom.

46

THE CONTINUANCE OF THE PHYSICAL SEED OF ABRAHAM

Though it is allowed by all conservative expositors of Scripture that Abraham had a physical seed, and in particular that Jacob was the father of the twelve tribes of Israel, an examination of this evidence serves to provide a basis for the theological implications which are based upon this fact. To be sure, modern liberals have asserted that the accounts of Abraham and his posterity are only traditional myths, but as this is done only by sweeping denial of the authority of Scripture, it does not require refutation in a discussion with orthodox scholars who accept the inspiration of the Bible. If the record of Scripture is valid, there can be little question concerning the fact that Isaac was born as a son to Abraham and Sarah when they both were past age, by miraculous intervention of God. Nor is there much question concerning the fact that Isaac had the twin boys Esau and Jacob. Much of the content of the book of Genesis deals with the story of Jacob, the birth of the twelve patriarchs, and the beginning of Israel's history as such. Even unbelievers in Scriptural revelation will acknowledge that the modern Jew is a descendant of Jacob and recognize the historical sequence which has brought Israel to the present hour.

It should also be evident from Scripture and history that Israel is more than just a race. From the time they left Egypt they assumed the proportions of a great nation and, though for a time they lived with little political unity during the period of the judges, there is abundant evidence to sustain the rise of the nation under Saul, David, and Solomon. Their moral deterioration, the Assyrian and Babylonian captivities, and the regathering and restoration of Israel recorded in the books of Ezra and Nehemiah and supported by Zechariah and Malachi provide a setting for the New Testament. When Christ was born, Israel was a nation even though it was under the heel of Roman oppression.

With the destruction of Jerusalem, however, and the scattering of the children of Israel, their national characteristics were blurred for many centuries. It is of tremendous significance, however, that the ties which bound together the race of Israel were of such character that in our modern day the nation Israel has once again returned to its ancient land, established itself as a political state, and is recognized as such by most of the civilized world. In any ordinary meaning of the term, Israel has continued as a nation and is in existence today in that capacity.

The Promises to Israel As a Nation

Much of the evidence which supports the concept of Israel as a nation is bound up in the promises which are given to her which will be discussed later. Sufficient for the present purpose, however, is to point out that the original Abrahamic covenant expressly promised that God would make a great nation out of Abraham's seed (Genesis 12:2). To this nation is given the promise of possession of the land, which implies national characteristics.

Relative to the express question concerning the perpetuity of Israel as a nation, the promise given to Abraham in Genesis 17:7, 8 is of special importance. Here the covenant with Abraham is declared to be an everlasting covenant, and the land is promised to Israel as an everlasting possession. It would be of course impossible for the covenant to be everlasting and the possession of the land to be everlasting unless the nation also continued forever. The Hebrew expression for "everlasting" is *olam*, meaning "in perpetuity." While it might not quite be the equivalent of the infinite term "everlasting," it would certainly mean continuance as long as this present earth should last. It is the strongest expression for eternity of which the Hebrew language is capable. Inasmuch as these promises are reiterated to Isaac and to Jacob and are constantly referred to throughout the Old Testament, the nature of these promises confirms the continuance of Israel as a nation.

The matter of Israel's regathering, judgment, and restoration still to be fulfilled will be the subject of later discussion, and only can be anticipated here. It follows, however, that if the Scriptures teach Israel is to be regathered, brought back to their ancient land, and actually possess the area promised by God to Abraham in Genesis 15:18-21, these predictions in their very character would demand Israel's continuance as a nation. Inasmuch as these promises do not rest on a few isolated texts, but on hundreds of prophecies in the Old Testament which directly or indirectly anticipate a future day of glory for Israel, it is hardly too much to say that there are few doctrines that are better attested in the Bible than that of the future of Israel, provided that these prophecies are interpreted in their normal and literal sense.

THE EXPRESS PROMISES OF ISRAEL'S PERPETUITY AS A NATION

In addition to the strong predictions of Genesis 17, the most pointed pronouncements are made elsewhere in the Old Testament concerning Israel's continuance as a nation. One of these, which should be decisive in itself, is that expressed by Jeremiah at a time of Israel's apostasy and captivity. In this context of Israel's disintegration Jeremiah predicts a new covenant with the house of Israel and the house of Judah (Jeremiah 31:31) which will replace God's covenant with them in the Mosaic law (Jeremiah 31:32). After defining the millennial situation in which this covenant will be fulfilled for the nation Israel, Jeremiah adds this word of assurance: "Thus saith Jehovah, who giveth the sun for a light by day, and the ordinances of the moon and of the stars for a light by night, who stirreth up the sea, so that the waves thereof roar; Jehovah of hosts is his name: If these ordinances depart from before me, saith Jehovah, then the seed of Israel also shall cease from being a nation before me for ever. Thus saith Jehovah: If heaven above can be measured, and the foundations of the earth searched out beneath, then will I also cast off all the seed of Israel for all that they have done, saith Jehovah" (Jeremiah 31: 35-37).

In view of the fact that some amillenarians contend that the Abrahamic promise concerning Israel is conditioned on their obedience and therefore is set aside upon disobedience, it is most significant that this strongest prophecy in the Old Testament for the continuance of Israel is given in a setting when Israel is manifestly in apostasy and about to be carried off into captivity. It would be difficult to provide a setting anywhere which would make it clearer that this is God's sovereign purpose entirely apart from Israel's worthiness and the fulfillment is determined solely by God's power and will. As long as the sun and moon endure and as long as the heavens have not been measured, Israel will continue as a nation. The divine purpose to continue the nation Israel is supported by the continuance of these elements of natural creation as long as the present earth exists. It is not simply that they will continue as a seed, but as Jeremiah expresses it, Israel shall not cease "from being a nation before me for ever."

The promise of Israel's perpetuity in the new covenant in Jeremiah 31 is supported by the provisions which are itemized: (1) It is designated a covenant with "the house of Israel, and with the house of Judah." The covenant is therefore limited to the descendants of Jacob. (2) It is a covenant designed to replace the Mosaic covenant also made only with Israel. As such it will be written "in their hearts" rather than on tables of stone. (3) The fulfillment of the covenant may be expected after "the time of Jacob's trouble" mentioned in Jeremiah 30:7. Jeremiah predicted in 31:28: "And it shall come to pass that, like as I have watched over them to pluck up and to break down and to overthrow and to destroy and to afflict, so will I watch over them to build and to plant, saith Jehovah." The time of fulfillment is further identified as the time of Israel's regathering, indicated in Jeremiah 30:10 and Jeremiah 31:8 and following. (4) The time of its fulfillment is described as a period when there will be universal knowledge of the Lord. Jeremiah speaks of this in these words: "And they shall teach no more every man his neighbor, and every man his brother, saying, Know Jehovah, for they shall all know me, from the least of them unto the greatest of them, saith Jehovah" (Jeremiah 31:34).

Isaiah referred to this same time in Isaiah 11:9 when he predicted: "For the earth shall be full of the knowledge of Jehovah, as the waters cover the sea." This was an especially strong prediction in view of the fact that both Isaiah and Jeremiah lived in a day when ignorance of the Lord prevailed and apostasy characterized Israel. The new covenant therefore is related to the future day of Israel's glorious kingdom on the earth. (5) The period of its fulfillment will be one of great spiritual blessing. God will be publicly identified with Israel, and Israel will be God's people. Their sins will be forgiven, and they will be the beneficiaries of God's wonderful grace. It should be obvious to any student of premillennial interpretation that all of these prophecies fit naturally and easily into the context of the millennial hope.

The new covenant is frequently mentioned elsewhere in the Old Testament. In Isaiah 61:8, 9, in a similar context speaking of Israel's tribulation followed by regathering and blessing, it is affirmed that the covenant will be everlasting. Jeremiah himself reaffirms the covenant in 32:37-40 and mentions its everlasting character and fulfillment in the time of Israel's regathering.

The Prophet Ezekiel repeats all the familiar elements found in earlier statements of the covenant, namely that Israel is to be regathered, to be reunited in one kingdom, to be ruled by one king, is to be forgiven and cleansed from idolatry, and will dwell forever in the land of their covenant of peace (Ezekiel 37:21-28). God is going to be present with them, and Israel will be known all over the world as a nation blessed of God.

Because these prophecies interpreted in their normal and natural way would unmistakably affirm the premillennial interpretation of prophecy, amillenarians deny these conclusions and usually hold that the new covenant as given to Israel is being fulfilled by the church today. Though this is quite foreign to the Old Testament presentation, they claim that the New Testament authorizes this transfer of promises from the nation to the church and that particulars such as the coming time of tribulation, regathering of Israel, their re-establishment in the land, their being ruled by one king, and being united as one nation must be interpreted spiritually as being fulfilled in the gathering out of the church from all nations into the one body of Christ. Before turning to other New Testament evidence confirming the continuance of Israel as a nation, attention must be directed to this amillennial interpretation of the new covenant.

There are five references in the best texts of the New Testament in which the term *new covenant (kaine diatheke)* is found (Luke 22:20; I Corinthians 11:25; II Corinthians 3:6; Hebrews 8:8; 9:15). In addition there are several other references which are properly within the sphere of this study as referring to the new covenant without the precise words being used (Matthew 26:28; Mark 14:24; Romans 11:27; Hebrews 8:10, 13; 10:16; 12:24). It is, of course, hardly possible to treat the subject adequately without a more prolonged discussion than can be undertaken here. A more complete presentation is afforded in *The Millennial Kingdom,* chapter 18, by the writer, and in Dr. J. Dwight Pentecost's *Things to Come,* chapter 8.

In regard to Israel's continuance as it relates to the new covenant, it is significant that only one passage specifically identifies the new covenant with that spoken of by Jeremiah. This is found in Hebrews 8. It is not too much to say that amillenarians who are careful scholars consider this passage one of the most important in their argument identifying the church with Israel.

The argument of Hebrews at this point is that Jesus Christ as our High Priest has a more excellent ministry and is the Mediator of a better covenant providing better promises than that of the Aaronic priesthood built on the Mosaic covenant. This is stated in Hebrews 8:6: "But now hath he obtained a ministry the more excellent, by so much as he is also the mediator of a better covenant, which hath been enacted upon better promises." The writer of Hebrews then proceeds to prove this by quoting the new covenant of

Jeremiah as demonstrating that the Mosaic covenant was faulty and needed to be replaced. He states in verse 7: "For if that first covenant had been faultless, then would no place have been sought for a second." He continues by quoting Jeremiah's new covenant with the words: "For finding fault with them, he saith, Behold, the days come, saith the Lord, that I will make a new covenant with the house of Israel and the house of Judah." Verses 9 through 12 are a quotation from the provisions of the new covenant given in Jeremiah 31. The writer of Hebrews then concludes in verse 13: "In that he saith, A new covenant, he hath made the first old. But that which is becoming old and waxeth aged is nigh unto vanishing away."

The interpretation of this quotation as it relates to the new covenant is complicated by the fact that conservative scholars have no less than five differing points of view, one of which is the amillennial interpretation. Briefly stated, these five positions are these: (1) The postmillennial interpretation that the promise of future blessing for the Jews will be fulfilled in the people of Israel in the latter days of the period of the church on earth when the Jews are converted and accept Christ as Saviour. This was typical of the conservative postmillennialism of the nineteenth century. (2) That the new covenant in both the Old and New Testaments concerns Israel and Israel alone and has no relationship specifically to Gentiles or the church. This was the viewpoint of Darby and is one of several premillennial approaches. (3) That the new covenant has a twofold application to the church in the present age and to Israel in the future millennial age. This view was popularized by the *Scofield Reference Bible*. (4) That there are in fact two new covenants, one for Israel to be fulfilled in the future, one for the church to be fulfilled in the present age, both founded upon the grace of God and the sacrifice of Christ. This view was supported by Lewis Sperry Chafer in his *Systematic Theology* and by Charles Ryrie in his book, *The Basis of the Premillennial Faith*. (5) The amillennial position that the church is true Israel and that the prophecies given to Jeremiah and other prophets are being fulfilled in the church age in a spiritualized way.

The postmillennial point of view has been largely discarded with a defunct postmillennialism and does not figure prominently in current eschatological discussions. Interpreters usually choose either between the amillennial point of view or one of the three premillennial interpretations. Darby's teaching that the new covenant both in the New and Old Testaments concerns Israel alone is not usually accepted by premillenarians, though it has many attractive arguments. The principal difficulty is that the Lord's Supper seems to relate a new covenant to the church which makes it difficult to confine the term to Israel's future. Usually the choice is between Scofield's position or that of Chafer in premillennial circles. For the purpose of our present discussion relative to the perpetuity of the nation Israel, it will suffice to show that the amillennial point of view is not that which is taught in Hebrews, though there are problems that remain in the premillennial understanding of this passage.

Oswald Allis defines the amillennial interpretation in these words: "For the gospel age in which we are living is that day foretold by the prophets when the law of God shall be written in the hearts of men (Jeremiah 31:33) and when the Spirit of God abiding in their hearts will enable them to keep it (Ezekiel 11:19, 36:26f)" (Prophecy and the Church, p. 42). He argues that the quotation before us in Hebrews 8 is a clear and unmistakable statement to this effect. Allis writes: "The passage speaks of the new covenant. It declares that this new covenant has already been introduced and that by virtue of the fact that it is called 'new' it has made the one which it is replacing 'old,' and that the old is about to vanish away. It would be hard to find a clearer reference to the gospel age in the Old Testament than in these verses in Jeremiah" (ibid., p. 154). An examination of the passage in Hebrews, however, does not support what Allis claims. Though the writer quotes the entire new covenant as given by Jeremiah, in his exegesis he uses only one word, namely, the word *new*. His argument in brief is based on the fact that Jeremiah predicted a new covenant in the Old Testament. This prediction proved that the Mosaic covenant was not intended to be an everlasting covenant and would in fact be done away. He does not say that Jeremiah's covenant is in effect now. While the New Testament in other passages alludes to the covenant of Jeremiah as in the quotation in Hebrews 10:16 and states that Jesus is the Mediator of a new covenant in Hebrews 12:24, nowhere in the New Testament is the church specifically put under the detailed provisions of the covenant of Jeremiah. The normal premillennial interpretation therefore considers these references (1) as an application of the general truth of the grace of God illustrated in the new covenant with Israel but also of the church, or (2) as two new covenants, one for Israel and one for the church. The problem yields to the patient exegesis of all passages relating to this subject in the New Testament, but even the New Testament, as in Romans 11:27, refers the detailed fulfillment of the covenant of Jeremiah to the second coming of Christ and the deliverance of Israel, a passage which amillenarians characteristically avoid as the plague. The amillennial point of view is the most extreme of the five possible viewpoints and is not supported by a careful study of the new covenant in the New Testament.

A study of further particulars in the New Testament related to the question of Israel's continuity serves to confirm that the word *Israel* is used in the New Testament in the same sense as in the Old and that promises to Israel continue to be inviolate, including their future restoration.

Amillenarians, while denying any future to Israel as a nation, are, however, divided as to whether Israel continues as a race. Allis follows the traditional amillennial approach in making Israel and the church one and the same as far as New Testament teaching is concerned. More recently amillenarians of both conservative and liberal backgrounds have tended to regard Israel as something distinct from the church. William Hendriksen, for instance, a well-known amillenarian, takes the position that Israel means Israel in the New Testament, not the church. In a similar way Charles Hodge, the postmillenarian of the last generation, held that the term *Israel* is never used in the New Testament except for those who were physical descendants of Jacob. It would seem in view of the fact that some amillenarians and postmillenarians concede that Israel means Israel in the New Testament it would be unnecessary to debate this point. However, in view of the evidence that many amillenarians consider it, as Allis does, "an almost unprecedented extreme" to insist that Israel actually means Israel (*Prophecy and the Church*, p. 218), it is necessary to dispose of this point first.

NEW TESTAMENT EVIDENCE

A study of the New Testament demonstrates beyond question that there is a continued contrast between Israel and Gentiles as such throughout the New Testament. Israel as a nation is addressed again and again after the beginning of the New Testament church in such passages as Acts 3:12; 4:8, 10; 5:21, 31, 35; 21:28, etc. A most significant illustration is Paul's prayer for Israel that they might be saved found in Romans 10:1 which is a clear reference to the use of the term *Israel* as a nation outside the church. The term *Jews*, derived from the tribe of Judah, is also used in I Corinthians 10:32. The argument of Paul in Romans 9 is certainly built on the idea of Israel as a separate nation. He surveys their peculiar promises and privileges in Romans 9:4, 5 and expresses the wish that he himself might be cursed if by this means his brethren, i.e., Israel, could be saved (Romans 9:3, 4).

Not only is Israel regarded as a separate nation, but Gentiles as such are expressly excluded. In Ephesians 2:12: "Ye [Gentiles] were at that time separate from Christ, alienated from the commonwealth of Israel, and strangers from the covenant of promise, having no hope and without God in the world." In the discussion which follows it is important to note that Paul does not indicate that Gentiles come into these promises given to Israel, but rather pictures both Jew and Gentile as being joined in an entirely new entity, namely, the body of Christ. The fact, therefore, that in the New Testament Israel and Gentiles are contrasted to each other is strong evidence that the term *Israel* continues to mean what it meant in the Old Testament, namely, the descendants of Jacob.

Perhaps more to the point in this discussion is the New Testament contrast between natural Israel and the church. As has been previously pointed out, there is a tendency on the part of some amillenarians to regard the church as the New Testament Israel. The New Testament in continuing the contrast between Israel and the church first of all notes that natural Israel — that is, unsaved Israelites — are not in the church. There is then no teaching that the nation of Israel as such becomes the church as such. Instead the nation Israel is promised a future, and, though this future is largely fulfilled by spiritual Israel, the existence of these promises as distinct from God's program for the church maintains the difference between the two terms.

A central passage in the New Testament on this point is found in Romans 11 where Paul raises the question that is before us: "I say then, Did God cast off his people?" (Romans 11:1). In his argument which follows he, first of all, answers this question in an absolute negative by asserting that there always has been a remnant of Israel and that there will be a remnant in the future. He notes the fact that the great majority in the nation Israel are spiritually blinded and that their hardness of heart has occasioned God's turning to the Gentiles in the present age. He anticipates, however, that this is a temporary situation which will be followed by a future blessing of the nation Israel. He states in Romans 11:15: "For if the casting away of them is the reconciling of the world, what shall the receiving of them be, but life from the dead?" He acknowledges that Israel at the present time is broken off from the olive tree or the place of divine blessing, but he predicts a future ingrafting of Israel into "their own olive tree" (Romans 11:24). This is to take place when Israel's blindness is lifted (Romans 11:25), which will be followed by the fulfillment of Israel's covenants and their restoration as a nation as indicated in Romans 11:26-32. This extended passage then expressly denies the contention that Israel has no future or continuance as a nation. The hope that is set before is not the hope given to the church which already is in the place of blessing in this present age and has no title to the promises given to Israel of possession of the land and other portions of their predicted future.

Not only is the nation Israel contrasted to the church, but spiritual Israel is contrasted to Gentile Christians who are in the body of Christ. This perhaps is the crux of the entire question, namely, are Gentile Christians ever designated Israelites? The argument of Romans 9:11 where this problem is expressly discussed makes clear that spiritual Israel and Gentile Christians continue to be contrasted. Spiritual Israelites never become Gentiles, and Gentile Christians never become Israelites. The statement of Romans 9:6, "For they are not all Israel, that are of Israel," does not deny this, but rather indicates that all who are physical descendants of Abraham do not necessarily inherit the spiritual promises. The contrast is between Israel according to the flesh and Israel which is spiritual, rather than a reference to Gentile believers. As has been previously pointed out, Gentile believers are the spiritual seed of Abraham who received the promise of blessing to all nations which was to come through Abraham. This does not mean, however, that they received the promises that came through Jacob to the nation of Israel.

Probably the most important text used by those who attempt to prove that Israel and the church are one is that found in Galatians 6:15, 16, which reads as follows: "For neither is circumcision anything, nor uncircumcision, but a new creature. And as many as shall walk by this rule, peace be upon them, and mercy, and upon the Israel of

God." It has been argued that the expression "Israel of God" is used here of the church as a whole.

It may be observed first that if this passage does use the term "Israel of God" for the church, it is the only passage in the entire New Testament where there is any evidence in the text for such a conclusion. Seen in the setting of its context, it is by no means the clear assertion that the church is the Israel of God as is sometimes claimed by its proponents. Paul is stating in these closing verses of the epistle to the Galatians the pre-eminence of the cross of Christ before which neither circumcision nor uncircumcision availed. The important fact is that those who trust in Christ who died for them become a new creature quite apart from any rite of circumcision or its lack. Upon those who have thus apprehended the grace of God and have been delivered from the law and its religious regulations, Paul breathes a benediction of peace and mercy. Then he adds, "And upon the Israel of God." The most natural explanation of this is that Paul is stating that anyone, whether Jew or Gentile, who walks by this rule is worthy of his benediction, but especially is this so for the Israel of God, i.e., Israelites who are the godly remnant of this age, that is, believers in the Lord Jesus Christ. The use of the Greek *kai* is best translated by the word *and* and only rarely is used in the sense of *even* as would be required if the term Israel of God is entirely equivalent to the expression "as many as walk by this rule." The passage does not state that the Israel of God and the church, i.e., the new creation, are coextensive. At the most, such identification is possible, but not probable. Paul's statement is simply a recognition of his particular interest in Israelites who have come to know Christ and expresses the hope that they would enter into the freedom of grace of which he is such an able exponent in the epistle to the Galatians.

One of the familiar arguments against the continuance of Israel as a nation is the idea that when Israel rejected Christ they failed to meet the necessary conditions for the fulfillment of their promises and are in fact disinherited as far as national promises are concerned. According to this point of view, an Israelite today has only the possibility of entering spiritually into the promises given to the church, not the promises given to Israel as a nation.

This question is largely answered by the materials already presented. The fact of continued recognition of Israel as a nation and the presentation of their future hope in Romans 11 would seem to be a sufficient answer. Two additional passages, however, may be considered.

In Matthew 21:43 Christ said in connection with the parable of the householder: "Therefore say I unto you, The kingdom of God shall be taken away from you, and shall be given to a nation bringing forth the fruits thereof." A casual examination of this text would seem to indicate the taking away of the kingdom of God from Israel. Even amillenarians, however, have seldom claimed this text, as a careful examination of it indicates quite another conclusion. First, those to whom He was addressing this verse were by no means the total of Israel. He could hardly say to the religious leaders of His day or to those within the hearing of His voice that their unbelief was sufficient to take away Israel's future hope from the nation as a whole. Second, the question can be raised — To what nation is the kingdom of God going to be given? Certainly no other people or race are any more qualified to receive the kingdom of God than the nation of Israel. Third, what did He mean by the kingdom of God?

This declaration of Christ is understood when it is interpreted as a statement that the scribes and Pharisees who rejected Christ, illustrated in the rejection of the son of the householder in the preceding parable, would never enter into the blessings of the kingdom of God. The term *nation* here should be understood as a people, i.e., anyone who would bring forth the fruits of faith. Some have interpreted the word *nation* here as referring to Israel, but to another generation of Israel, namely, the godly remnant of the future. Still others refer it to the church. It is probably better to leave it undefined as referring to any people who meet the conditions. In any case, the passage is not a proper basis for Israel's disinheritance. The Kingdom, as the sphere of divine blessing, is for all true believers.

A second major text in the New Testament has already been mentioned, namely, the question raised by Paul in Romans 11:1: "Did God cast off his people?" To this Paul gives a categorical negative in the words, "God forbid." He not only expressly denies that God has cast off Israel, but he argues that this has never been God's method with His people when they have sinned. While the unbelieving in Israel bore their judgment, as is true even in the present age, there was a continuing program for the godly remnant in Israel as illustrated in the present age as well as in the Old Testament. The argument of Romans 11, which has already been reviewed, comes to a climax in the expression "All Israel shall be saved" (Romans 11:26). This certainly does not mean all the church shall be saved, nor is it simply a reference to all the elect in Israel. It is rather, as many scholars have pointed out, the concept of Israel's national deliverance at the time of the second coming of Christ at which time they are saved from their persecutors and delivered from physical destruction. The contrast is between the individual salvation of Israel in the present age through faith in Christ and the collective deliverance of Israel at the end of the age.

SUMMARY

In this discussion three points of view concerning Israel's continuance as a nation have been considered: (1) The view that denies that Israel exists today, and therefore has no future. (2) The concept that Israel continues as a race, but not as a nation. (3) The premillennial interpretation that Israel has not only continuity as a race, but a future as a nation in the premillennial kingdom. It was shown that Israel's continuance as a nation depended first of all upon the nature of her promises as contained, for instance, in Genesis 17 where the Abrahamic covenant is declared to be everlasting and the land is promised to Israel as an everlasting possession. This was confirmed by the new covenant revealed by Jeremiah in which Israel was promised that it would continue as long as the moon endured. The New Testament interpretation of the new covenant was shown not to shake or alter this clear revelation in the Old Testament. New Testament evidence was cited to prove that Israel as a nation continues throughout the period of New Testament revelation. Israel continues to be addressed as a nation and is distinguished both from Gentiles and the church. Both the nation Israel is contrasted to the church as a whole and spiritual Israel is contrasted to Gentile Christians in the body of Christ. Miscellaneous texts and arguments such as Galatians 6:15, 16, Matthew 21:43, and Romans 11, when properly interpreted, would seem to confirm the conclusion that Israel is promised continuance as a nation throughout human history. The faithfulness of God to Israel is a convincing proof that God keeps His word whether to Israel or to the church, and in this we can rest our faith.

CHAPTER IV

THE PROMISE OF THE LAND TO ISRAEL

In the broad program of prophecy relating to Israel, few factors are more important than the promise to Abraham of the perpetual possession of the land. It is not only constantly reiterated in prophecies relating to the hope of Israel, but it is an integral part of the call to Abraham which begins the program. According to Genesis 12:1 God had said to Abraham: "Get thee out of thy country, and from thy kindred, and from thy father's house, unto the land that I will show thee." It is almost impossible to avoid the plain implication that the term *the land* was a geographic designation and that Abraham understood it in this way.

Practically all conservative expositors agree that Abraham was instructed in his original call to leave his native country, Ur of the Chaldees, and proceed to the land of Canaan. The historical record of his journey is recorded in Genesis 11:31: "And Terah took Abram his son, and Lot the son of Haran, his son's son, and Sarai his daughter-in-law, his son Abram's wife; and they went forth with them from Ur of the Chaldees, to go into the land of Canaan; and they came unto Haran, and dwelt there." After delay in Haran, still outside the land of Canaan, they finally entered the land itself after the death of Terah as recorded in Genesis 12:5: "And Abram took Sarai his wife, and Lot his brother's son, and all their substance that they had gathered, and the souls that they had gotten in Haran; and they went forth to go into the land of Canaan; and into the land of Canaan they came." The original call to Abraham, therefore, involved a geographic understanding and that to

Abraham the expression *the land* meant the land of Canaan promised to him and his seed.

It would seem redundant to cite these proofs if it were not for the fact that the term *the land* and its related promises are frequently spiritualized as if they had no geographic implications whatever. As has been pointed out in previous discussion, amillenarians usually follow one of two routes in evading the premillennial interpretations of this passage, namely, (1) that the promises of the land are to be spiritualized and relate to heaven; or (2) that the promises are to be interpreted literally but are conditional and will never be fulfilled. In order to consider the amillennial argument, it is necessary to examine first the promise of the land to the seed of Abraham as unfolded in the Old Testament; second, to study the dispossessions of the land involved in the three dispersions of Israel; third, to ascertain whether these promises have in some sense already been fulfilled or whether they are subject to future fulfillment; and, fourth, whether taking the evidence as a whole there is good ground for belief in the future fulfillment of these promises. Certain conclusions may then be drawn concerning Israel's prophetic hope.

The Promise of the Land to Abraham's Seed

In examining the promise of the land, it may be observed first that Abraham understood the promises of God as relating to the literal land of Canaan. This is demonstrated by his movement from Ur to Canaan as has already been pointed out. It is further confirmed by the promise in Genesis 12:7 given after his entrance into the land: "Unto thy seed will I give this land." Certainly Abraham understood it to refer to the physical land of Canaan. This is reinforced by his experience in Genesis 13 where after being separated from Lot he is urged to look northward, southward, eastward, and westward (Genesis 13:14). At that time God assured him: "For all the land which thou seest, to thee will I give it, and to thy seed for ever" (Genesis 13:15). Further, he is instructed: "Arise, walk through the

land in the length of it and in the breadth of it: for unto thee
will I give it" (Genesis 13:17). It is practically impossible
to evade understanding these verses as referring to the literal
land.

In Genesis 15:18-21 the exact dimensions of the land
are given and the territory is described as running from
the river of Egypt, which was the borderline between Egypt
and Canaan, and the great river, the river Euphrates, hundreds of miles to the east. It becomes clear from the description which follows which itemizes the heathen tribes
occupying this territory that God had in mind more than
just the small area occupied by the Canaanite himself, but
rather the entire area between these two boundaries. Here
again it is obvious Abraham understood that a large geographic area was involved.

The New Testament comments on this expectation of
Abraham in Hebrews 11:8, 9 where it is written: "By faith
Abraham, when he was called, obeyed to go out unto a
place which he was to receive for an inheritance; and he
went out, not knowing whither he went. By faith he became a sojourner in the land of promise, as in a land not
his own, dwelling in tents, with Isaac and Jacob, the heirs
with him of the same promise." So far, all must agree that
a literal land is in view. Amillenarians are quick to point
out, however, that verse 10 goes on to say: "For he looked
for the city which hath the foundations, whose builder and
maker is God." Also, in Hebrews 11:16 it adds: "But now
they desire a better country, that is, a heavenly: wherefore
God is not ashamed of them, to be called their God; for he
hath prepared for them a city."

Do these allusions to a heavenly city nullify the idea
of a literal land? A careful study of this passage will demonstrate that the subject is Abraham's faith. His faith first of
all was in regard to the land, and his faith was indicated
by his obedience and his sojourning in the land in tents. The
same faith which he manifested in God's promise concerning
the land is also manifested in Abraham's faith concerning the heavenly city. The land represented God's promise

in relation to time, more specifically, the future kingdom of Christ on earth, while the heavenly city has to do with eternity, the New Jerusalem and the new earth. In the case of both, Abraham never possessed in life the fulfillment of the promises and like others he died in faith before the promises were fulfilled. The fact that Abraham believed both the temporal promises of God and the eternal promises of God does not lead to the conclusion that the earthly promise and the heavenly promise are one and the same. It is rather that they require the same attitude of faith. The major emphasis of Scripture, however, is on Abraham's belief in the temporal promises of God and to this the Scriptures constantly refer. The allusions to the eternal state and Abraham's expectation and faith are in fact rare, while the promises relating to possession of the land are one of the major themes of the Old Testament.

In presenting the Messianic hope, Isaiah, in the major passage of Isaiah 11:1-12, after describing the justice which will characterize the land when the Messiah reigns, prophesies the regathering of the children of Israel "from Assyria, and from Egypt, and from Pathros, and from Cush, and from Elam, and from Shinar, and from Hamath, and from the islands of the sea." He goes on to state that He is going to "gather together the dispersion of Judah from the four corners of the earth." The whole context makes clear that they are being brought back to the land.

Similar passages abound in Isaiah. For instance, in Isaiah 14:1 it is declared: "For Jehovah will have compassion on Jacob, and will yet choose Israel, and set them in their own land." According to Isaiah 27:13 the children of Israel are going to be gathered from Assyria and Egypt and "they shall worship Jehovah in the holy mountain at Jerusalem." This of course involves a return to the land.

In Isaiah 43:5-7 the regathering of Israel to the land is described: "Fear not; for I am with thee: I will bring thy seed from the east, and gather thee from the west; I will say to the north, Give up; and to the south, Keep not back; bring my sons from far, and my daughters from the end of the earth; every one that is called by my name, and whom I have created for my glory, whom I have formed, yea, whom I have made." It is stated categorically in Isaiah 60:21: "Thy people also shall be all righteous; they shall inherit the land for ever."

The book of Isaiah concludes with a great prophecy concerning the regathering of Israel as it will be consummated when they are brought from the ends of the earth to the Promised Land in the beginning of the millennium. According to Isaiah 66:20: "And they shall bring all your brethren out of all the nations for an oblation unto heaven, upon horses, and in chariots, and in litters, and upon mules, and upon dromedaries, to my holy mountain Jerusalem, saith Jehovah, as the children of Israel bring their oblation in a clean vessel into the house of Jehovah."

This theme of Israel is continued in Jeremiah 16:14-16: "Therefore, behold, the days come, saith Jehovah, that it shall no more be said, As Jehovah liveth, that brought up the children of Israel out of the land of Egypt; but, As Jehovah liveth, that brought up the children of Israel from the land of the north, and from all the countries whither he had driven them. And I will bring them again into their land that I gave unto their fathers. Behold, I will send for many fishers, saith Jehovah, and they shall fish them up; and afterward I will send for many hunters, and they shall hunt them from every mountain, and from every hill, and out of the clefts of the rocks." It should be noted that the regathering of Israel to their ancient land is here described as being a regathering to the last man, something that was not remotely approached in any previous return.

In describing the time of the great tribulation in Jeremiah 30:1-7, it is declared in verse 3: "For, lo, the days come, saith Jehovah, that I will turn again the captivity of my people Israel and Judah, saith Jehovah; and I will cause them to return to the land that I gave to their fathers, and they shall possess it." It is further stated in Jeremiah 30:10, 11: "Therefore fear thou not, O Jacob my servant, saith Jehovah; neither be dismayed, O Israel: for, lo, I will save thee from afar, and thy seed from the land of their captivity; and Jacob shall return, and shall be quiet and at ease, and none shall make him afraid. For I am with thee, saith Jehovah, to save thee: for I will make a full end of all the nations whither I have scattered thee, but I will not make a full end of thee; but I will correct thee in measure, and will in no wise leave thee unpunished." In Jeremiah 31 the return of Israel to the land is predicted in verse 5: "Again shalt thou plant vineyards upon the mountains of Samaria; the planters shall plant, and shall enjoy the fruit thereof." The regathering is described in Jeremiah 31:8: "Behold, I will bring them from the north country, and gather them from the uttermost parts of the earth, and with them the blind and the lame, the woman with child and her that travaileth with child together: a great company shall they return hither."

In the description of the new covenant in Jeremiah 31:31-40 it is predicted that Israel will return to the land and that Jerusalem will be built in a certain area which had formerly never been used for building purposes. It is remarkable that this precise area has been built into a portion of the modern city of Jerusalem in fulfillment of this prophecy.

Another clear reference to the regathering of Israel and their being planted in their land is found in Jeremiah 32:37-44. In verse 37 it is stated: "Behold, I will gather them out of all the countries, whither I have driven them in mine anger, and in my wrath, and in great indignation; and I will bring them again unto this place, and I will cause them to dwell safely." Again, in verse 41 it is declared: "Yea, I will rejoice over them to do them good, and I will plant them in this land assuredly with my whole heart and with my whole soul." Jeremiah promises that they will again possess the fields in and about Jerusalem and that God will cause their captivity to return. In Jeremiah 33, God solemnly swears that He will cause their captivity to return, that justice and righteousness will be executed in the land, and that the seed of David will reign on the throne. Such passages could be multiplied, such as Ezekiel 11:14-21 where in verse 17 God says plainly: "I will give you the land of Israel."

Ezekiel 20:33-38 describes the judgment upon Israel at the beginning of the millennial kingdom, when the rebels are prohibited from entering the land in contrast to the righteous who do. In Ezekiel 20:42 it is written: "And ye shall know that I am Jehovah, when I shall bring you into the land of Israel, into the country which I sware to give unto your fathers." Again in Ezekiel 34:13 God promises: "And I will bring them out from the peoples, and gather them from the countries, and will bring them into their own land; and I will feed them upon the mountains of Israel, by the watercourses, and in all the inhabited places of the country."

In the great prophecy concerning the valley of dry bones in Ezekiel 37 the significant statement is given in verses 21, 22: "And say unto them, Thus saith the Lord Jehovah: Behold, I will take the children of Israel from among the nations, whither they are gone, and will gather them on every side, and bring them in to their own land: and I will make them one nation in the land, upon the mountains of Israel; and one king shall be king to them all; and they shall be no more two nations, neither shall they be divided into two kingdoms any more at all." Ezekiel adds in verses 24, 25 that David is going to reign over them. In verse 25 he writes: "And they shall dwell in the land that I have given unto Jacob my servant, wherein your fathers dwelt; and they shall dwell therein, they, and their children, and their children's children, for ever: and David my servant shall be their prince for ever."

The process of the regathering of Israel is declared in Ezekiel 39:25-29 to extend to the whole house of Israel and indicates that they will be brought back into their land to the last man, as stated in verse 28: "And they shall know that I am Jehovah their God, in that I caused them to go into captivity among the nations, and have gathered them unto their own land; and I will leave none of them any more there." The meaning of this passage is that they will be gathered to their land and that God will not allow a single Israelite to remain in dispersion. This has never been fulfilled by any previous regathering.

Most of the minor prophets continue this prophetic strain, so prominent in Isaiah, Jeremiah, and Ezekiel. The undying love of God for Israel is declared in Hosea, and, though according to 3:4 the children of Israel will be without a king and a priesthood, they are assured in verse 5: "Afterward shall the children of Israel return, and seek Jehovah their God, and David their king, and shall come with fear unto Jehovah and to his goodness in the latter days." The Prophet Joel, after declaring the judgment of God upon Israel, closes his book by declaring: "But Judah shall abide for ever, and Jerusalem from generation to generation" (3:20).

The Prophet Amos, after an almost unrelieved indictment on Israel for their sin, closes his book with five verses in chapter 9 beginning in verse 11, where it is affirmed that the tent of David which is fallen will be raised up again. The abundance of crops is described and Amos declares God's intention in verses 14 and 15: "And I will bring back the captivity of my people Israel, and they shall build the waste cities, and inhabit them; and they shall plant vineyards, and drink the wine thereof; they shall also make gardens, and eat the fruit of them. And I will plant them upon their land, and they shall no more be plucked up out of their land which I have given them, saith Jehovah thy God." This major passage on the regathering of Israel is significant because it pictures the revival of Israel after divine judgment upon them, the abundant crops that will characterize Israel in those days, and closes with the assurance that they will no more be scattered once they are brought back to the land. Here again is a prophecy which was not fulfilled in previous regatherings and demands a future regathering in which this prophecy will be completely fulfilled. It is to this prophecy that James alludes in Acts 15:15-18 when he declared at the council of Jerusalem that it was the divine order that there should be blessing on the Gentiles first and that this was to be followed by the restoration of Israel and the rebuilding of the tent of David.

Obadiah continues this strain on the regathering of Israel when he writes in verse 17: "But in mount Zion there shall be those that escape, and it shall be holy; and the house of Jacob shall possess their possessions." In that day according to verse 21: "the kingdom shall be Jehovah's."

Micah gives a comprehensive picture of the future Messianic kingdom in 4:1-8. Israel is pictured in their ancient land in peace and security, regathered from their former scattered position and sitting under their vines and fig trees in safety. The book concludes with these words: "Thou wilt perform the truth to Jacob, and the lovingkindness to Abraham, which thou hast sworn unto our fathers from the days of old" (7:20).

The remaining minor prophets continue this theme. Zephaniah closes chapter 3 with the picture of Israel regathered and rejoicing in the Lord in their ancient land. Zechariah speaks at length on the future blessings of Israel, describing the streets full of happy children in Zechariah 8:5 and Israel is being regathered from the east and from the west in chapter 8:7, 8. Jerusalem is pictured as the capitol of the earth in 8:22. The regathering of Israel is mentioned specifically in Zechariah 10:10 where Israel is described as gathered out of Assyria and Egypt. The concluding chapter of Zechariah, beginning as it does with the second coming of Christ, pictures the changes in the land in the millennial kingdom and the wealth and prosperity and spiritual blessing of Israel. All of these prophecies imply that the promises of the land are going to be fulfilled and Israel will once again be established in the area promised to the seed of Abraham.

The careful analysis of these many promises relative to Israel's possession of the land and their regathering from the ends of the earth makes clear certain important principles. First, as intimated in previous discussion, the land, though subject to delay and Israel's temporary dispossession, is

promised unconditionally to the seed of Abraham. Its ultimate possession is therefore based on the grace principle
rather than the law principle. Second, it should be evident that the promise of the land is not given to Gentiles,
but to the physical seed of Abraham; to be sure, not all the
seed, but nevertheless to be fulfilled literally by the future
generation of Israelites on earth at the time of the second
coming of Christ. Third, the title of the land is declared
to be unending in its character. By this we should understand that the land belongs to Israel as long as the present
earth endures. Fourth, not only is the title to be given forever, but the land is actually to be possessed as long as the
earth endures, once it is given to Israel at the beginning of
the millennial kingdom. Fifth, it is clear that the promises
are geographic and that the boundaries announced in Genesis 15 will have specific application when Israel is finally in-
stalled in their land in the millennial period. Only by in-
discriminate spiritualization of all the terms and promises
relating to the land can these prophecies be nullified. The
fact that they are stated and restated so many times in so
many different periods of Israel's history, even in times of
apostasy and departure from God as in the days of Jeremiah and Ezekiel, and by so many of the minor prophets
makes clear that God intended them to be taken at their
face value.

THE DISPOSSESSIONS OF THE LAND

Though only premillenarians insist that Israel is eventually to possess the Promised Land and fulfill literally the
promises pertaining thereto, it is agreed by all that Israel
in the course of its past history has suffered three major
dispossessions. Jacob and his family voluntarily went to
Egypt at Joseph's invitation to avoid the famine and thereby
left the land promised to Abraham's seed. In Egypt they
sojourned for many generations until the time of the Exodus.
After the return to the land under Moses and Joshua, the
children of Israel lived for hundreds of years within the
general area promised to Abraham, but never possessing it
in its entirety even in the most extended period of the

kingdom under Solomon. The moral disintegration which followed Solomon and the division of the kingdom of Israel into two kingdoms ultimately resulted in the second dispersion, first, in the captivity of Assyria beginning in 721 B.C. and then in the later captivity of the two remaining tribes following the invasion by Babylon beginning in 606 B.C. The second dispersion is the subject of prophecy by Moses in Deuteronomy 28:62-65 and is mentioned in Deuteronomy 30:1-3. At the same time there were frequent promises of restoration from this dispersion as indicated in the prophecies already cited in Jeremiah. The return after the second dispersion is indicated specifically by Jeremiah in chapter 29:10, 11 where the prediction is given that after seventy years they would be able to return to Jerusalem.

The third and final dispersion began in A.D. 70, with the destruction of Jerusalem and the desecration of the entire land which followed in the next century. From this dispersion, Israel has begun to return in the twentieth century as witnessed in the establishment of the nation Israel. Two million of these people are now established in their ancient land. The present regathering being witnessed by our generation is the largest movement of the people of Israel since the days of Moses, and may be understood to be the beginning of that which will be completed subsequent to the second coming of Christ and the establishment of His kingdom on earth.

The principles involved in the dispersion and regathering of Israel are sometimes called the Palestinian covenant. This is outlined in particular in the final message of Moses in Deuteronomy, chapters 28, 29, and 30. According to Deuteronomy 28:63-68, Israel was warned that they would be scattered over the face of the earth if they departed from God. Along with this, however, it was anticipated that there would be a future return in which a godly remnant of Israel would repent. This is stated explicitly in Deuteronomy 30:1-3: "And it shall come to pass, when all these things are come upon thee, the blessing and the curse, which I have set before thee, and thou shalt call them to mind among all the nations, whither Jehovah thy God hath driven thee, and shalt return unto Jehovah thy God, and shalt obey his voice according to all that I command thee this day, thou and thy children, with all thy heart, and with all thy soul; that then Jehovah thy God will turn thy captivity, and have compassion upon thee, and will return and gather thee from all the peoples whither Jehovah thy God hath scattered thee."

This regathering is connected with the return of Christ mentioned in Deuteronomy 30:3 and involves the restoration and regathering of all the children of Israel scattered over the face of the earth including righteous Israelites who have died and gone to heaven. As stated in Deuteronomy 30:4: "If any of thine outcasts be in the uttermost parts of heaven, from thence will Jehovah thy God gather thee, and from thence will he fetch thee." According to Deuteronomy 30:5-9, they are promised that they will be regathered to their land, restored spiritually, delivered from their enemies, and abundantly blessed. Though the prophecy is given in a context which conditions fulfillment on the future repentance of Israel, both this Scripture and many others relating to the regathering of Israel predict that Israel will repent and will therefore be restored and regathered.

The dispossessions of the land, therefore, are temporary judgments upon the generations of Israel who turned from God. While they lost possession of the land in the captivities and suffered as the Scriptures prophesied, at the same time God abundantly declares in His Word that their dispersion was temporary and their regathering is the ultimate purpose of God. Confirming this judgment is the dramatic fact of Israel's return to the land in our day after many centuries of dispersion, persecution, and affliction.

HAS THE PROMISE OF THE LAND ALREADY BEEN FULFILLED?

Generally speaking, amillenarians who deny that Israel will possess the Promised Land in the future tend to ignore the promises to the contrary in the Major and Minor Prophets and in many cases do not even attempt to offer evidence that these promises are conditional or are to be interpreted in a nonliteral way. Occasionally, however, some arguments are offered in the attempt to sustain the thesis that the promises have already been fulfilled in historic possessions of the land. George L. Murray for instance, in his book *Millennial Studies,* page 27, offers I Kings 4: 21-24 as evidence. It is stated in verse 21: "And Solomon ruled over all of the kingdoms from the River unto the land of the Philistines, and unto the border of Egypt: they brought tribute, and served Solomon all the days of his life." In I Kings 4:24 this same thought is continued: "For he had dominion over all the region on this side the River, from Tiphsah even to Gaza, over all the kings on this side the River: and he had peace on all sides round about him."

A careful study of this passage in the light of its context, however, will demonstrate that, while Solomon ruled over all this area, he did not possess it, inasmuch as the kings are indicated as continuing their rule even though they paid tribute and served Solomon. The area was therefore not incorporated in the kingdom of Solomon, but rather came under his sway in the sense that the nations paid tribute and were at peace with Solomon. If this portion had been incorporated into the kingdom of Solomon, it would not have involved the kings' remaining on their thrones and paying tribute to him.

A similar argument is offered by Murray in reference to Joshua 21:43-45 where it is stated: "So Jehovah gave unto Israel all the land which he sware to give unto their fathers; and they possessed it, and dwelt therein." On the face of it this would seem to be a plain declaration that they did possess all the land. This promise, however, has to be limited by subsequent Scriptures. According to Judges 1:21 the Benjamites did not conquer the Jebusites. According to Judges 1:27, the children of Manasseh did not conquer all of their territory, and in verse 28 it is stated: "And it came to pass when Israel was waxed strong, that they put the Canaanites to taskwork, and did not utterly drive them out." In the verses which follow are itemized the areas which

Ephraim, Zebulun, Asher, and Naphtali did not possess. In other words, the statement of Joshua 21:43-45 must be understood as teaching that God on His part was faithful, but that the children of Israel did not enter into their possession.

Much later in Israel's history Murray notes that Nehemiah refers to the promise given to Abraham relative to the land and states, "Thou . . . hast performed thy words; for thou art righteous" (9:8). This must be understood in the same sense as Joshua in that indeed God did "give them the land," but they never possessed it historically in the Old Testament period.

The passages already cited relative to Israel's regathering and possession of the land are in themselves a complete refutation of this idea that Israel has already possessed the land in the past in its entirety. If the promise of the land was fulfilled in Joshua's time or in Solomon's, why do the many Scriptures later appeal to a future possession? Even though it may be conceded that the reference in Nehemiah is late in Israel's history, it by no means proves that the promises pertaining to the last regathering and establishment of Israel in the land have been fulfilled. In fact, it is quite to the contrary as we examine the context of Nehemiah.

There are three essentials to the fulfillment of the original promises given to Abraham regarding the possession of the land. First, the land must be actually possessed, that is, occupied, not simply controlled. Second, the possession must continue as long as the earth lasts, i.e., forever. Third, the land during this period of possession must be under the rule of the Messiah in a time of peace, tranquillity, and blessing. Nothing in history fulfills the many promises given to the prophets and, if it be judged that these promises must be fulfilled literally and surely, there remains only one possible conclusion — that is, that Israel in some future time will possess their promised land, including the entire area described in Genesis 15.

ARGUMENTS FOR FUTURE FULFILLMENT OF THE PROMISE

In reviewing the material already presented relative to Israel's future possession of the land, it may be seen that this is integral in the whole prophetic scheme involving the millennial kingdom, the return of Christ, and the consummation of the ages. The ground for fulfillment lies first in the nature of the promises themselves rooted as they are in the original proposition made to Abraham to leave his father's land and to go to a land that God would show him. The promises originally given to Abraham are reiterated again and again and form the backbone of Old Testament prophetic revelation. The promise of the land sustained Abraham, Isaac, and Jacob as they contemplated the future of their seed. The promise of the land was that which dominated Moses and Joshua as they brought the children of Israel from Egypt to the land. The hope of regathering was that which sustained Jeremiah and Ezekiel at the time of the captivities and Israel's moral apostasy. It formed the basis of their hope in future restoration both spiritually and politically. It has been further noticed that the very statement of the promises, though linked with a future repentance of Israel, is stated as certain and sure. It is linked with the perpetuity of the seed of Abraham which is promised continuance as long as the sun and moon endure.

The strongest kind of promises are related to the possession of the land in that not only the nation Israel is promised eternal continuity, but the land is promised as an everlasting possession. The emphatic description of the land given in Genesis 15:18-21 almost defies spiritualization, including as it does the heathen tribes which possessed it at the time the promise was given. The fact that Israel has been dispossessed of the land in three periods of its history is by no means an argument against ultimate possession, for imbedded in the very promises of dispossession are the promises that Israel will return and repossess the land. It has been demonstrated that these promises were not fulfilled in the past. Though Solomon temporarily controlled the area described by Abraham, he did not possess it and he did not occupy it. The prophets following Solomon certainly did not understand that Solomon had fulfilled the promise of the land and therefore promised future fulfillment. While God had been faithful, as witnessed by Nehemiah, it should be obvious to all that in Nehemiah's day the promises of possession of all the land were not fulfilled.

On every hand, therefore, an examination of the promises of the land of Israel supports the eschatology of Israel as a whole and the premillennial interpretation of the Scriptures. By so much also any spiritualization of Israel which would require fulfillment to the church in the present age or which would look to fulfillment in the eternal state would undermine not only the eschatology of Israel, but the program of eschatology as a whole. It is therefore not too much to say that the subject of the eschatology of Israel is a determinative one in the theology of future things, and as one decides these important questions he therefore decides the validity of eschatology in its broader scope. Inasmuch as the promises relating to Israel pervade the entire Scriptures, by so much a disclaiming of the promises given to Israel affects one's theology as a whole. It is for this reason that this subject is important, not only in the study of Israel itself, but in the establishment of premillennial theology.

SUMMARY

The theological implications of the promise of the land to Israel have been shown to be central in God's eschatological purpose for His ancient people. The promise of the land was integral in the original covenant with Abraham and was understood by him in a literal way. This is demonstrated in the constant reiteration of the promise in which literal possession of the land is implied or stated. The countless promises of the Old Testament which relate to the promise of the land were considered seriatim in a representative way. Such major passages as Isaiah 11, 14, 43, 60, 66, Jeremiah 16, 30, 31, 32, 33, Ezekiel 11, 20, 34, 37, 39, Hosea 3, Joel 3, Amos 9, Obadiah, Micah 4, Zechariah 8, and 10 were cited. Certainly this is an overwhelming proof that the entire Old Testament lends its confirmation to a promise of future possession of the land to Israel. These promises, though subject to delay and temporary dispossession, were never transferred to Gentiles but were declared to be unending in character, its title given forever with specific boundaries announced in Genesis 15 to Abraham himself.

The dispersions predicted when Israel was out of the land were prophesied, but it was demonstrated that not only were the dispersions fulfilled, but also the regathering. Evidence was adduced that the final regathering will include every Israelite to the last man, a promise which today has never been fulfilled.

The amillennial argument that the promise of the land was fulfilled in Solomon's day was refuted by the fact that Solomon never fulfilled the promise in any proper sense, and that subsequent Scriptures regarded the promise as subject to future fulfillment. Assertions of Joshua and Nehemiah to the fact that God had fulfilled all His promises to Israel were found to be limited by the context to the thought that God had kept His Word though Israel had failed to possess the land. The arguments for future fulfillment of the promise hang therefore on the certainty of the Word of God. Just as the prophecy concerning Israel has always had its fulfillment in the past, so it will also in the future. Israel's promise of the land is just as sure as the Christian's promise of heaven.

CHAPTER V

THE KINGDOM PROMISED TO DAVID

In the study of the prophecy relating to Israel, one of the major themes is the kingdom promised to David. In this aspect of prophecy converge the other principal elements of Israel's predicted future. The promise to Abraham concerning his seed and the land, and the frequent prophecy of Israel's ultimate regathering are part of a larger pattern which promises a future kingdom to Israel.

First intimations of a future kingdom are found in the promises given to Abraham in Genesis 17:6 where it is recorded: "And I will make thee exceeding fruitful, and I will make nations of thee, and kings shall come out of thee." This is restated in verse 16 of the same chapter in relation to the promise of the son of Sarah: "And I will bless her, and moreover I will give thee a son of her: yea, I will bless her, and she shall be a mother of nations; kings of peoples shall be of her." The promise of a kingdom given to Abraham's seed is subsequently narrowed to Isaac and Jacob, and in Genesis 49:10 is further limited to the tribe of Judah. Jacob in his prophetic summary of the future of Israel prophesied concerning Judah: "The sceptre shall not depart from Judah, nor the ruler's staff from between his feet, until Shiloh come; and unto him shall the obedience of the peoples be." Though the full significance of this passage has been debated by some scholars, it can hardly be disputed that it limits the throne to Judah and his descendants. It may be concluded therefore that early in Israel's history the concept of a future kingdom constituted the matrix for Israel's eschatology.

The subject of the kingdom as it relates to Israel is so large that it will be possible to survey only some of its principal characteristics. Four areas will be considered: first, the covenant with David; second, Old Testament confirmation; third, New Testament confirmation; fourth, prophetic fulfillment.

THE COVENANT WITH DAVID

In understanding the promises of a future kingdom given to Israel, one of the major Scriptures is that containing the Davidic covenant recorded in II Samuel 7 and I Chronicles 17. In this covenant the promise of a king and a kingdom is narrowed to David's seed.

According to the context, David had been concerned that the worship of the Lord had centered in the tabernacle, a tent-like structure, which had been originally built by Moses. David himself had built permanent houses for his family, and he felt it was unfitting for the worship of God to center in such a temporary structure. Accordingly, he called in Nathan the prophet and said to him: "See now, I dwell in a house of cedar, but the ark of God dwelleth within curtains." Nathan responded as recorded in II Samuel 7:3: "Go, do all that is in thy heart, for Jehovah is with thee." That night the Lord corrected Nathan the prophet in reminding him that God had never commanded them to build Him a house of cedar. Nathan was instructed to deliver a message to David, the substance of which was that God would build a house to David in the sense of a posterity and that his son, yet to be born, would build a temple for the Lord.

The provisions of the covenant are given in II Samuel 7 beginning in verse 11: "Moreover Jehovah telleth thee that Jehovah will make thee a house. When thy days are fulfilled, and thou shalt sleep with thy fathers, I will set up thy seed after thee, that shall proceed out of thy bowels, and I will establish his kingdom. He shall build a house for my name, and I will establish the throne of his kingdom for ever. I will be his father, and he shall be my son: if he commit iniquity, I will chasten him with the rod of men, and with the stripes of the children of men: but my

lovingkindness shall not depart from him, as I took it from
Saul, whom I put away before thee. And thy house and thy
kingdom shall be made sure for ever before thee: thy throne
shall be established for ever."

The promise given to David includes the following
provisions: (1) David is promised a child who would suc-
ceed him on the throne. (2) The temple which David
desired to build would be constructed by this son. (3) The
throne of his kingdom would be continued forever and would
not be taken away from David's son even if he committed
iniquity. (4) In summary, the prophet declared that David's
house, kingdom, and throne would be established forever.
Part of these promises were fulfilled in Solomon in that
Solomon was later born and ultimately built the temple.
The promise goes far beyond Solomon, however, in that
the kingdom, throne, and David's house itself were established forever. There seems to be little disposition to
question that Solomon is the son mentioned in the covenant
and that he built a literal temple as a house for the Lord.
The difficulties in interpretation come in examining the exact
meaning of the term *house* as it pertains to David's posterity and the words *throne* and *kingdom*.

By way of preliminary definition, it would seem only
natural to assume that by the term *throne* was meant
the political rule of David over Israel. It was assured that
a future king over Israel would come from David's line.
This is the meaning of the promise that David's house would
continue forever. The term *kingdom* is probably the
most difficult term to define, but it would seem quite clear
to David that God was referring to his own rule over Israel
in a political sense. This is confirmed by David's own remarks in connection with the giving of the covenant. He
understood the promise meant that his house would continue forever. David addresses Jehovah in II Samuel 7:
18, 19: "Who am I, O Lord Jehovah, and what is my house,
that thou hast brought me thus far? And this was yet a small
thing in thine eyes, O Lord Jehovah; but thou hast spoken
also of thy servant's house for a great while to come; and

this too after the manner of men, O Lord Jehovah!" David
after recounting Israel's history adds this word in verse
25: "And now, O Jehovah God, the word that thou hast
spoken concerning thy servant, and concerning his house,
confirm thou it for ever, and do as thou hast spoken." In
similar vein he concludes in verse 29: "Now therefore let
it please thee to bless the house of thy servant, that it may
continue for ever before thee; for thou, O Lord Jehovah,
hast spoken it: and with thy blessing let the house of thy
servant be blessed for ever."

OLD TESTAMENT CONFIRMATION OF THE COVENANT

It is probable that there would be little question about
the meaning of this covenant, if it did not involve eschatology
as a whole. It would seem that the promises are simple and
direct that David's posterity should continue forever and
that his political kingdom would not end. However, even
such a simple interpretation presents some immediate problems, as David himself seems to anticipate when he notes
that the prophecy concerns a long time to come.

The principal difficulty, however, seems to be that the
connotation of the Davidic covenant supports the premillennial interpretation of the Bible involving a future
reign of Christ on earth as David's greater Son. This point
of view is quite unacceptable to the amillenarian and therefore for them some interpretation of the Davidic covenant
must be found other than that of a literal fulfillment. Generally speaking, amillenarians deny that this covenant has
any decisive force on the millennial question and find its
terms fulfilled in the present day with God's dealings with
the church. Quite often the attempt is made to deny that
anything in the Old Testament construes a premillennial
eschatology and statements are made such as that of Louis
Berkhof: "The only Scriptural basis for this theory [i.e., pre-
millennialism] is Revelation 20:1-6, after an Old Testament content has been poured into it" (*Systematic Theology*,
p. 715).

In brief, the amillennial point of view is that the Davidic

kingdom promised to David's posterity is not a rule over
the house of Israel, but a spiritual rule over the saints fulfilled in Christ's present session at the right hand of God.
Such an idea of course is not contained in the Davidic
covenant as it is recorded in II Samuel 7, but it is asserted
that later Scriptures give this interpretation. For this reason the implications of the provisions of the Davidic covenant can be determined only after ascertaining the interpretation placed upon this covenant by other Old Testament
Scriptures. Then a further step must be taken of examining
the New Testament treatment of the same subject. Though
this can be done only briefly within the limits of our present
discussion, some important facts can be cited which de-
cisively determine the ultimate interpretation of the Davidic
covenant.

The covenant with David is not only given twice in its
major content — namely, II Samuel 7 and I Chronicles 17
— but it is also confirmed in Psalm 89. In this and other Old
Testament references there is no allusion anywhere to the
idea that these promises are to be understood in a spiritualized sense as referring to the church or to a reign of God
in heaven. Rather, it is linked to the earth and to the seed
of Israel, and to the land. According to Psalm 89:3, 4 Jehovah declares: "I have made a covenant with my chosen,
I have sworn unto David my servant: Thy seed will I establish for ever, and build up thy throne to all generations."
This concept is declared again later in the same psalm
beginning in verse 29 where it is promised that the seed will
endure forever in spite of the specific problem of Israel's
sins and departure from God. It is affirmed unalterably that
God is going to fulfill His Word to David regardless of what
his seed does: "His seed also will I make to endure for
ever, and his throne as the days of heaven. If his children
forsake my law, and walk not in mine ordinances; if they
break my statutes, and keep not my commandments; then
will I visit their transgression with the rod, and their iniquity
with stripes. But my lovingkindness will I not utterly take
from him, nor suffer my faithfulness to fail. My covenant

will I not break, nor alter the thing that is gone out of my lips. Once have I sworn by my holiness: I will not lie unto David: his seed shall endure for ever, and his throne as the sun before me. It shall be established for ever as the moon, and as the faithful witness in the sky" (Psalm 89:29-37). According to this psalm the covenant concerns David, his physical seed, and the relationship of his rule to the children of Israel. There is no indication that this kingdom extended to a spiritual entity such as the church nor that the throne in view is the throne of God in heaven rather than the throne of David on earth.

In the well-known prophecy concerning the birth of Christ given in Isaiah 9:6, 7 it is stated again that the throne of David is in view: "For unto us a child is born, unto us a son is given; and the government shall be upon his shoulder: and his name shall be called Wonderful, Counsellor, Mighty God, Everlasting Father, Prince of Peace. Of the increase of his government and of peace there shall be no end, upon the throne of David, and upon his kingdom, to establish it, and to uphold it with justice and with righteousness from henceforth even for ever. The zeal of Jehovah of hosts will perform this." Again the throne of David is mentioned specifically and the promise indicates that the fulfillment will go on forever.

In Jeremiah 23:5, 6 the reign of the king who is the son of David is described as coming to pass in a day when Judah and Israel shall be saved and dwell safely. Jeremiah writes: "Behold, the days come, saith Jehovah, that I will raise unto David a righteous Branch, and he shall reign as king and deal wisely, and shall execute justice and righteousness in the land. In his days Judah shall be saved, and Israel shall dwell safely; and this is his name whereby he shall be called: Jehovah our righteousness." In the verses immediately following, this reign is linked with the regathering of the children of Israel and their occupation of their ancient lands. Jeremiah writes in Jeremiah 23:7, 8: "Therefore, behold, the days come, saith Jehovah, that they shall no more say, As Jehovah liveth, who brought up the children of Israel out of the land of Egypt; but, As Jehovah liveth, who brought up and who led the seed of the house of Israel out of the north country, and from all the countries whither I have driven them. And they shall dwell in their own land."

It is certainly extreme spiritualization to take the regathering of Israel as an equivalent of the outcalling of the church and the execution of "justice and righteousness in the land" as being a reference to the rule of Christ in heaven, as amillenarians would need to interpret the passage. This is another strong confirmation that the literal interpretation of the Davidic covenant was intended.

In Jeremiah 30:8, 9 another reference is found to the reign of the seed of David and again it is in a context of Israel's future regathering which will be consummated following the great tribulation. According to Jeremiah 30:9, 10 it is predicted that Israel will be free from Gentile oppression and will serve the Lord and David their king. Jeremiah writes: "But they shall serve Jehovah their God, and David their king, whom I will raise up unto them. Therefore fear thou not, O Jacob my servant, saith Jehovah; neither be dismayed, O Israel: for, lo, I will save thee from afar, and thy seed from the land of their captivity; and Jacob shall return, and shall be quiet and at ease, and none shall make him afraid." As in other passages, the fulfillment of the Davidic covenant is linked with the return of Israel to the land following their time of Jacob's trouble, as indicated in the preceding context. Here it is stated that they will serve Jehovah and David their king. There is no good reason for not taking this exactly as it is written, namely, that David will be raised from the dead and will with Christ reign over the people of Israel in the millennium. Even if David is understood to refer to Christ as David's greater Son, it is still a clear reference to a future millennium rather than to a situation that exists today.

A similar confirmation is found in Jeremiah 33:14-17 where the same particulars are spelled out in detail. Jeremiah writes: "Behold, the days come, saith Jehovah, that I will perform that good word which I have spoken concerning the house of Israel and concerning the house of Judah. In those days, and at that time, will I cause a Branch of righteousness to grow up unto David; and he shall execute justice and righteousness in the land. In those days shall Judah be saved, and Jerusalem shall dwell safely; and this is the name whereby she shall be called: Jehovah our righteousness. For thus saith Jehovah: David shall never want a man to sit upon the throne of the house of Israel." The context concerns itself with Israel's restoration and specifically speaks of the house of Israel and the house of Judah. Mention again is made that righteousness and justice will exist in the land and that Judah will be in the land and Jerusalem will be in safety. Such a situation does not prevail in this present age and is not related here or elsewhere to the reign of Christ from the throne of His Father in heaven.

It would seem hardly necessary to cite all the additional passages that might be available, but, inasmuch as this subject has been controverted, the mass of Old Testament prophecies that deal with the subject certainly give added stature to the literal interpretation of the Davidic covenant. Ezekiel 37:22-25 indicates that Israel in that future day will have one king over them and will be a people of God. In verses 24 and 25 Ezekiel writes: "And my servant David shall be king over them; and they all shall have one shepherd: they shall also walk in mine ordinances, and observe my statutes, and do them. And they shall dwell in the land that I have given unto Jacob my servant, wherein your father dwelt; and they shall dwell therein, they, and their children, and their children's children, for ever: and David my servant shall be their prince for ever." It should be obvious that in Ezekiel's days David had been dead over four hundred years and that this is a prophecy that David will be raised from the dead prior to the millennial reign of Christ and share with Christ the rule of the people of Israel. Such a situation is quite foreign to the present age.

One of the problems which is often raised concerning

the fulfillment of the Davidic covenant is the fact that for many years the throne was unoccupied. From the time of the Babylonian captivity on there was no literal earthly kingdom. This, however, is taken into full consideration in the Word of God. According to Hosea 3:4, 5, written long before the Babylonian captivity, it was predicted: "For the children of Israel shall abide many days without king, and without prince, and without sacrifice, and without pillar, and without ephod or teraphim: afterward shall the children of Israel return, and seek Jehovah their God, and David their king, and shall come with fear unto Jehovah and to his goodness in the latter days." According to this passage, therefore, it can be assumed that God, while permitting the throne to be empty, nevertheless assured it to David and his seed prophesying Israel would return to the Lord, i.e., in the future millennial kingdom and resurrected David would be their king.

It is also promised in Amos 9:11 that the tabernacle of David would be restored in the latter days, apparently another reference to the revival of the political kingdom of Israel over which David was king. Further light will be cast upon this passage in the study of the New Testament confirmation. A concluding word is found in Zechariah 14 where it is predicted that after the second coming of Christ when His feet will touch the Mount of Olives (Zechariah 14:4), and "Jehovah shall be king over all the earth" (Zechariah 14:9). This of course is not a contradiction of the fulfillment of the Davidic covenant, but is a part of the same picture.

As far as the Old Testament narrative is concerned, the prophets are clear in these multiplied passages that God anticipated a literal fulfillment of His promise to David. It would seem evident, therefore, that the people of Israel were acting in good faith when they expected God to revive their kingdom, deliver them from their enemies, and restore them to their ancient land. Such as was their expectation when Christ came the first time, and such can be their expectation at His second coming.

NEW TESTAMENT CONFIRMATION

It has been demonstrated that the Old Testament clearly predicts a future kingdom in which David and his posterity would rule over the children of Israel regathered and dwelling in their ancient land. Amillenarians, however, have countered this evidence by their assertion that the New Testament interprets these predictions as being fulfilled in the present age. Before turning, therefore, to some of the theological arguments in support of an eschatology for Israel, some of the New Testament evidence should be examined.

One of the first texts dealing with this subject is found in the announcements of the angel to Mary that she is to be the mother of Christ. In this connection she is told that Christ will reign on the throne of His father David over the house of Jacob. According to Luke 1:30-33 the angel said: "Fear not, Mary: for thou hast found favor with God. And behold, thou shalt conceive in thy womb, and bring forth a son, and shalt call his name JESUS. He shall be great, and shall be called the Son of the Most High: and the Lord God shall give unto him the throne of his father David: and he shall reign over the house of Jacob for ever; and of his kingdom there shall be no end." In the light of the prominence given this same subject in the Old Testament, the question may be fairly raised: What would such a prophecy mean to Mary? For any Jewish maiden who accepted the Old Testament prophecy concerning the future of Israel and entertained the hope of a coming Messiah, would hardly question that the prophecy given by the angel would be interpreted literally, that is, she would understand by the throne of David an earthly throne such as David enjoyed in his lifetime.

Further, it is declared that Mary's Son would reign over the house of Jacob forever. Mary certainly would not understand by the phrase "the house of Jacob" a reference to saints in general regardless of racial background. To her it could mean only one thing and that is the descendants of Jacob, namely, the twelve tribes of Israel. Inasmuch as this would be the normal and natural understanding on the part of Mary in such a prophecy, it is almost unthinkable that God would have used this terminology if as a matter of fact the hope of Israel was a mistake and the prophecies given in the Old Testament were not intended to be understood literally.

It seems quite clear that the disciples anticipated much the same kind of a literal fulfillment. According to Matthew 20:20-23, the mother of James and John came to Christ with a request concerning them: "Command that these my two sons may sit, one on thy right hand, and one on thy left, in thy kingdom." She certainly was not asking that these disciples would share the Father's throne in glory, but it is obvious that what she anticipated was that they would share the earthly rule of Christ in the kingdom promised to Israel. Though Christ refused the request on the ground that only the Father had the right to bestow such an honor, He did not deny that such an honor might be afforded someone, which would hardly have been the case if the throne of God itself had been in view. In any case, Christ did not tell her that her request was out of bounds because there was to be no earthly rule. It was rather that it was improper to obtain such an honor as a requested privilege.

It is entirely possible that the request originated in the incident recorded in Matthew 19 where Christ had promised them in verse 28: "Verily, I say unto you, that ye who have followed me, in the regeneration when the Son of man shall sit on the throne of his glory, ye also shall sit upon twelve thrones, judging the twelve tribes of Israel." Here Christ is specifically confirming the concept of a future kingdom in which Israel would be the subjects and in which the disciples would have part in the government. If indeed the Old Testament prophecies were not intended to teach a rule of God from heaven over saints on earth, the language of this prediction would be misleading.

As late as Luke 22 on the night before His crucifixion, Christ said to His disciples in verses 29, 30: "I appoint unto you a kingdom, even as my Father appointed unto me, that ye may eat and drink at my table in my kingdom; and ye shall sit on thrones judging the twelve tribes of Israel." Thus, late in His life after He had already been rejected by the people of Israel Christ repeats the same promises which had characterized the Old Testament, the announcement to Mary, and His conversation with His disciples on previous occasions. There was going to be a kingdom over Israel and the disciples would sit on thrones participating in the government.

A final confirming word is given by Christ in connection with His ascension in Acts 1. Here it is recorded that the disciples came to Christ and asked the question according to Acts 1:6: "Lord, dost thou at this time restore the kingdom to Israel?" From the question itself it becomes apparent that the disciples were still anticipating an earthly kingdom and hoped for its immediate realization. In reply to them, Christ did not say that their hope was vain, that there was not going to be a literal fulfillment. Rather He replied: "It is not for you to know the times or seasons, which the Father hath set within his own authority." By so much, He was affirming that the kingdom would be fulfilled, but that the time was not for them to know. In the verses which follow He directs their attention to the task that was immediately before them, and to the power of the Spirit which would aid them in the world-wide proclamation of the gospel. He said in effect that before the kingdom could come there had to be a fulfillment of God's purpose in the church. The consummation of the prophecies regarding the kingdom therefore was postponed, but not cancelled. The kingdom on earth is consistently interpreted in a literal way and is not spiritualized in the narratives dealing with the subject in the gospels and Acts.

One of the important passages in the New Testament bearing on this subject is found in Acts 15:14-18. Here in the council in Jerusalem the question had been raised concerning the status of the Gentiles in the present age. It was difficult for the Jews to understand that for the time being the Gentiles should have a place of equality with Israel, in view of the many prophecies in the Old Testament which anticipated Israel's pre-eminence and glory. In the settlement of this problem it is recorded that James made the following address: "Brethren, hearken unto me: Symeon hath rehearsed how first God visited the Gentiles, to take out of them a people for his name. And to this agree the words of the prophets; as it is written, After these things I will return, and I will build again the tabernacle of David, which is fallen; and I will build again the ruins thereof, and I will set it up: that the residue of men may seek after the Lord, and all the Gentiles, upon whom my name is called, saith the Lord, who maketh these things known from of old." The passage concludes with the suggestion that Gentiles be not obligated to keep Jewish customs except in cases where this might hinder fellowship with the Jews, and winning them to Christ.

Of major importance is the main thesis of his remarks which is based on a reference and partial quotation of Amos 9:11, 12. Scholars have not agreed on the precise interpretation of this passage and amillenarians in particular have labored to make this a contradiction of the premillennial point of view. However, it seems that "after these things I will return" refers to the return of Christ after the period of Gentile prominence which began in 606 B.C. and is destined to continue until the second coming. It is after these things — i.e., judgment on Israel, their scattering, and discipline — that Christ will return and build again the tabernacle or tent of David. The reference to the tent of David, of course, does not concern itself with any building as such but rather with the political power and sway which David enjoyed.

That the rebuilding of the tabernacle of David is the restoration of the kingdom to Israel and not the construction of the church in the present age is borne out by the prophecies that are related to it in Amos, which have already been noted in a previous discussion. Amos 9:14 reads as follows: "And I will bring back the captivity of my people Israel, and they shall build the waste cities, and inhabit them; and they shall plant vineyards, and drink the wine thereof; they shall also make gardens, and eat the fruit of them." In other words, the kingdom concerns itself with the rule over the people of Israel in their ancient land which will be characterized by revival and restoration, exactly what we would expect by the reference to rebuilding the tent of David. This is further confirmed by the final verse of Amos 9: "And I will plant them upon their land, and they shall no more be plucked up out of their land which I have given them, saith Jehovah thy God." In other words, the kingdom is related to the time when Israel will be regathered and be established in their ancient land. The normal and natural exegesis of these passages therefore requires a future restoration to Israel and a future fulfillment of the kingdom promises. The divine order therefore is judgment on Israel and blessing upon Gentile first, to be followed by judgment on Gentile and blessing on Israel. This is not only the order of the Old Testament, but it is the order of this portion in Acts and is further confirmed by the order indicated in Romans chapter 11 where Israel is to be grafted back into the place of blessing which Gentiles now enjoy.

The consummating Scripture of course in the New Testament which puts the capstone on all these indications is found in Revelation 20 where it is stated plainly that Christ will rule for 1000 years. His rule is marked off by certain events which occur before and certain events which follow His millennial reign. The claim of the amillenarian that Revelation 20 is the only passage in the Bible which teaches an eschatology for Israel is certainly not sustained by the abundant evidence which has been cited from both the Old and New Testaments.

Is the Covenant to Be Interpreted Literally?

With the Scripture testimony before us, it is now possible for us to consider some of the problems which exist in this interpretation. It has already been pointed out that postponement and delay of the kingdom is by no means an

argument against it, for Hosea 3:4, 5 anticipates precisely
such a situation. Further, the long years in which no one
was on the throne of David did not hinder the angel from
assuring Mary that her Son would sit on the throne. As in
other promises of God, delay and postponement does not
affect the certainty of the ultimate fulfillment.

Probably the leading question in the entire argument
is whether a literal fulfillment of these promises is to be
expected. This of course faces frontally the whole premil-
lennial-amillennial argument which can only be resolved
on the relative cogency of the results of the methods. Amillenarians, generally speaking, tend to spiritualize promises
which would teach a future millennium, though they interpret literally prophecies which do not interfere with their
system. Premillenarians, on the other hand, believe that
prophecy is not a special case requiring spiritualization any
more than any other area of divine revelation and they
believe also that prophecy should be interpreted normally
— that is, in an ordinary, grammatical and literal sense unless the context or theology as a whole plainly indicates to
the contrary. Premillenarians do not find the amillennial
charge — that the premillennial position is untenable, self-
contradictory, and hopelessly confused — is sustained. While
obviously the premillennial system of interpretation has
much more detail than the amillennial denial, and even
though there are countless minor problems, the major elements of the premillennial system have seemed quite cogent
to thousands of careful Bible students and scholars. The
question of literal interpretation therefore cannot be brushed
aside *a priori* as if the literal interpretation of prophecy
is impossible. Rather, there are sound and good arguments
to the contrary.

George N. H. Peters in his *Theocratic Kingdom* provides
a masterly summary of the arguments in favor of literal
interpretation. In his proposition 52, he lists 21 arguments
in favor of literal interpretation and includes other col-
lateral material. These can be summarized under ten arguments for literal interpretation: "(1) The solemn char-

acter of the covenant which was confirmed by an oath. (2) A spiritual fulfillment would not be becoming to a solemn covenant. (3) Both David and Solomon apparently understood it to be literal (II Samuel 7:18-29; II Chronicles 6:14-16). (4) The language used, which is also used by the prophets, denotes a literal throne and kingdom. (5) The Jews plainly expected a literal fulfillment. (6) The throne and kingdom as a promise and inheritance belong to the humanity of Christ as the seed of David rather than belong to His deity. (7) There is no ground for identifying David's throne and the Father's throne. (8) A symbolical interpretation of the covenant leaves its interpretation to man. (9) The literal fulfillment is requisite to the display of God's government in the earth, necessary to the restoration and exaltation of the Jewish nation and deliverance of the earth from the curse. (10) Literal fulfillment is necessary to preserve the Divine unity of purpose" (cf., *Millennial Kingdom*, by the writer, p. 199). These arguments, usually ignored by amillenarians, have great weight and seem to provide a reasonable approach to the Davidic covenant and the promise of the kingdom.

The matter of literal fulfillment of the promises is confirmed also by the fact that certain portions of it have been literally fulfilled. One of these is in the birth of Christ Himself who literally fulfilled many promises pertaining to David's seed. Here the meticulous accuracy of the promises given to David and Solomon is illustrated. In the covenant as originally given there is a careful distinction between the seed of David, the seed of Solomon, and their respective thrones. In the covenant David is assured that his seed will reign forever, while Solomon is only promised that his throne will continue forever. In this fine point is an illustration not only of the literalness of the prophecy, but of God's intention to cut off Solomon's line at the time of the captivity of Judah embodied in the declarations in Jeremiah 22:20 and 36:30. In the New Testament in the lineage of Christ as recorded in Matthew 1 and Luke 3, it seems to be made evident that Joseph descended from

Solomon, which line was cut off, while Mary descended from Nathan, another son of David, rather than from Solomon. This point of view not only confirms the necessity of the virgin birth, that is, that Joseph could not be the father of Christ, but also supports the idea that God intended the prophecy embodied in the covenant with David to be taken literally even to such a fine distinction.

This literal interpretation and expected fulfillment of the Davidic covenant is of course in keeping with the other covenants previously studied. Certainly it fits in beautifully with the idea that the Abrahamic covenant anticipates Israel continuing eternally as a nation and possessing the land forever. The possession of the land is limited by the continuance of the earth itself and terminates with the destruction of the heavens and the earth at the end of the millennium. The force of the Hebrew, however, is that Israel will continue to possess the land perpetually, that is, until eternity begins.

The assertion of amillenarians that the Davidic throne is simply a reference to God's throne in heaven is not supported by either the Old or the New Testament prophecies relating to the future of Israel. Of the 59 references to David in the New Testament, there is not one connecting the Davidic throne with the present session of Christ. Such an inference could be established only by spiritualizing many prophecies both in the Old and New Testaments.

Samuel H. Wilkinson, in his book, *The Israel Promises and Their Fulfillment*, pp. 56, 57, has given a forceful summary of this point. "Nevertheless, facts are stubborn things. It is a fact that God has declared that Israel is not to cease from being a nation before Him for ever. It is a fact that the Jewish nation, still in unbelief, survivor of all others, alone retains its national identity. . . . It is a fact that the promise of a land (the territorial limits of which were defined) to the posterity of Abraham, as also the promise of a son of David's own line to occupy David's throne for ever, were *unconditional* promises, ratified by covenant and oath. It is a fact that the posterity of Abraham has never yet fully possessed and enjoyed the whole of the land so granted and that no son of David occupies David's throne. . . . The O. T. promises are all as certain of fulfillment in their O. T. sense and meaning and purpose to Israel, as are the N. T. promises certain of fulfillment to the Church." A study of the Old and New Testament therefore seems to confirm a genuine eschatology for Israel involving their continuity as a nation, their regathering and restoration to their ancient land, and their enjoyment of a kingdom in which Christ will reign over them. David resurrected from the dead will share this position of authority as a prince under Christ. Such an interpretation not only provides a literal fulfillment of many prophecies pertaining to it, but is fully honoring to the Word of God as that which is inspired infallibly by the Holy Spirit.

THE FUTURE PROGRAM OF ISRAEL IN RELATION TO THE KINGDOM

On the basis of prophecy which has already been fulfilled and prophecies which can be expected to be fulfilled in the future, a broad future program for Israel can be established in the Bible. This anticipates that the regathering of Israel, begun in the twentieth century, will be continued. If the rapture of the church may be assumed to be pretribulational, Israel's program will unfold immediately after the church is translated. With the realignment of nations, Israel will enter into a covenant with the Gentile rulers of the Middle East, as anticipated in Daniel 9:26, 27. A covenant will be signed for a period of seven years, which will be the last seven years of Daniel's 490 years allotted to Israel. During the first half of this seven years Israel will enjoy prosperity. Orthodox Jews will apparently revive their ancient sacrifices and a temple will be provided. After three and one-half years of the covenant have run their course, it will be abruptly broken, in keeping with the predictions of both the Old and New Testaments and especially the words of Christ in Matthew 24:15-22. A period of great trouble which Jeremiah refers to as "the time of Jacob's trouble" will follow. Israel will be persecuted, and their only hope will be to escape their enemies by hiding. The period of great tribulation will feature not only a time of trouble for Israel, but will be a period in which divine wrath is expressed on the earth. Great judgments will take place including warfare, earthquakes, famines, and stars falling from heaven. According to the book of Revelation, the majority of the earth's population will be destroyed in these catastrophes. A major world war brings the period to a close. As Christ returns from heaven, He descends to the Mount of Olives and delivers His persecuted people. The precise situation is described in Zechariah 14 and Revelation 19 and is confirmed in Romans 11:26, 27.

With the destruction of the enemies of Christ and the establishment of the millennial kingdom, the process of Israel's regathering and restoration will be completed. According to Ezekiel 20:34-38, regathered Israel will be judged and rebels or unbelievers will be purged out. Only those who pass the searching judgment of Christ are allowed to enter into the millennial period. These are brought back to their ancient land and possess the area from the River of Egypt to the river Euphrates. Over this land Christ will rule as He rules over the entire world. David who is raised from the dead along with Old Testament saints has a part in the government of the people of Israel. This will also be shared by the twelve apostles, whom Christ assured participation in His government of Israel in the millennial state.

During the thousand-year reign of Christ, the remnant nation Israel, surviving the great tribulation, will greatly increase as will the Gentile nations, and repopulate the earth and rebuild their cities. At the end of the millennial reign of Christ, Satan is loosed and divine judgment overtakes any born in the millennium who rebels against Christ, who are Jewish and Gentile unbelievers. Though all the details are not supplied, it seems clear that the saints living on earth at the end of the millennium will be translated into their eternal state. The new heaven and the new earth will be created. The heavenly city, the New Jerusalem, will descend and rest upon the new earth. The description of the new earth given in Revelation 21:22 seems clearly to include Israel as well as Gentile saints of all ages. It is interesting to note, however, that the people of Israel retain their identity as Israelites even as the Gentiles retain their identity as Gentiles in the eternal state. Though there are distinctions depending on their backgrounds, all alike enjoy the presence of the King of kings and the countless blessings that belong to the eternal state.

The future of Israel is the fulfillment of a divine purpose sovereignly conceived in which the children of Israel constitute one of the major vehicles of divine revelation. Through them God gave the Scriptures and through them God has illustrated many of His attributes, especially those of His faithfulness, love, and righteousness. Inasmuch as Israel has not only a prominent place in the plan of God for the past, but also in the future, a proper understanding of the eschatology of Israel does much to open up a proper understanding of God's purpose as a whole and is seemingly indispensable to any detailed exegesis of the eschatology unfolded in the Old and New Testaments.

SUMMARY

The provisions of the covenant of David therefore form a broad platform for the eschatology of Israel embodied in the Davidic kingdom. It would seem that this covenant assured to David that his political rule as well as his physical posterity would continue forever even though it might be interrupted, just as the possession of the land was temporarily interrupted. The covenant with David is confirmed not only by its dual revelation in II Samuel 7 and I Chronicles 17, but by the major confirmation of Psalm 89 and by many additional prophecies in the Old Testament such as Isaiah 9:6, 7; Jeremiah 23:5-8; 30:8-10; 33:14-17; Ezekiel 37: 22-25; Hosea 3:4, 5; Amos 9:11, 15, and similar Old Testament passages. New Testament confirmation was found in such major passages as Luke 1:30-33; Matthew 19:28; 20:20-

23; Luke 22:29, 30; Acts 1:6; 15:14-18; and the climactic prophecy of Revelation 20. The massive arguments for literal interpretation of these promises were presented as a proper basis for the fulfillment of this covenant in the future. On the expectation involved in the fulfillment of the Davidic covenant, a future program of Israel can be outlined, including God's dealing with Israel in the time of tribulation, to be followed by their blessing in the millennial reign of Christ and ultimate enjoyment of the eternal state in the New Jerusalem. The eschatology of Israel in a word depends on the authority and accuracy of Biblical prophecy and the legitimacy of its normal and literal interpretation.

CHAPTER VI

THE SUFFERING OF ISRAEL

The predicted suffering of Israel is one of the major aspects of Biblical prophecy concerning the future of this people. It is paradoxical that the nation chosen for exaltation and selected to be a special means of divine revelation should also be destined for suffering which would exceed that of any other nation of the world.

CAUSES OF ISRAEL'S SUFFERING

The trials of Israel stem from the basic conflict between divine purpose and satanic opposition. The very fact that God selected Israel as a special means of divine revelation makes the nation the object of special satanic attack. Satanic hatred of the seed of Abraham is manifested from the beginning of God's dealings with Abraham and continues through the entire course of human history culminating in the rebellion at the end of the millennium.

Spiritual warfare in relation to Israel is in evidence from the beginning. The fulfillment of God's purpose of bringing Abraham from Ur of Chaldees to the Promised Land was delayed and thwarted by Abraham's incomplete obedience in bringing his father and nephew Lot with him. Entrance to the land was delayed until his father died, and Lot continued to be a hindrance to him until he and Abraham separated. Satanic opposition to fulfillment of God's purpose in Abraham is also revealed in the delayed birth of Isaac, and only the miraculous intervention of God made it possible for Him to fulfill His prophecy of a seed to Abraham through whom He would bless the nations. In the case of Isaac, a similar situation is evident in the fact that only after years of supplication was a seed granted to Isaac and Rebekah. When Jacob and Esau were born, it was expressly an answer to prayer. The corrupting influence of Satan is manifest in both the lives of Esau and Jacob, and only by the grace of God was Jacob rescued from his compromising position. Jacob's life ended in Egypt, to which he had fled to avoid the famine, with none of his family remaining in the Promised Land. The subsequent experience of Israel in Egypt, where for a time they enjoyed prosperity but eventually were threatened with extermination, is well known to every student of the Bible. Only by divine intervention was Israel brought from Egypt to the Promised Land, and then only after years of failure and wandering in the wilderness.

The incomplete possession of the land, the spiritual degeneracy which characterized the time of the judges, and the apostasy that followed the days of Solomon are given large place in the Old Testament. In every particular Satan sought to spoil, to hinder, and to mar the purpose of God in the elect nation. The scattering of Israel in the captivities, the attempt recorded in the book of Esther to exterminate the Jew, and the ultimate capstone of satanic opposition to Israel's place of spiritual leadership was recorded in the gospels. In the New Testament, Israel's rejection of her Messiah is related, with Israel's resulting dispersion following the Roman persecution A.D. 70-135. Undoubtedly one of the principal causes for Israel's suffering has been the unending opposition of Satan to the fulfillment of God's purpose in the nation.

Coupled with Israel's failures as recorded in the Scriptures is the fact of divine discipline exercised on the nation. Israel was not only to be the channel of divine revelation of God, but also the example of God's faithfulness to a sinning people who are the objects of His love and grace. Accordingly, many pages of the Old Testament are dedicated to giving the sacred records of God's dealings with His wandering people. The studies of Israel's sufferings will illustrate this basic reason for the sufferings inflicted on the nation.

The sufferings of Israel, while revealing God's discipline and righteousness, are also demonstrations of His love. Joined to every righteous judgment upon Israel are many manifestations of divine grace in preserving a godly remnant, in giving them that which is far greater than they deserved and fulfilling His divine purpose in and through them in spite of their own failure and Satan's efforts to hinder the purpose of God. There is a majestic drama in the whole sequence of events that relate to Israel's history, and they epitomize to some extent the conflict between good and evil which is the basic Christian philosophy of history. The sufferings of Israel, therefore, should be seen in the context of satanic persecution, of divine discipline for sin, and of divine faithfulness to His chosen people.

THE SUFFERING OF ISRAEL IN FULFILLED PROPHECY

Early in the recorded history of Israel intimations are given of the fact that Israel would suffer. Moses solemnly warned the children of Israel in Deuteronomy 4:25-28 that God would bring them into suffering for their sins: "When thou shalt beget children, and children's children, and ye shall have been long in the land, and shall corrupt yourselves, and make a graven image in the form of anything, and shall do that which is evil in the sight of Jehovah thy God, to provoke him to anger; I call heaven and earth to witness against you this day, that ye shall soon utterly perish from off the land whereunto ye go over the Jordan to possess it; ye shall not prolong your days upon it, but shall utterly be destroyed. And Jehovah will scatter you among the peoples, and ye shall be left few in number among the nations, whither Jehovah shall lead you away. And there ye shall serve gods, the work of men's hands, wood and stone, which neither see, nor hear, nor eat, nor smell."

In the verses which immediately follow, however, hope is held out to Israel that if they will seek the face of God they will find forgiveness and restoration. In Deuteronomy

4:29, 30 Moses assured them: "But from thence ye shall seek Jehovah thy God, and thou shalt find him, when thou searchest after him with all thy heart and with all thy soul. When thou art in tribulation, and all these things are come upon thee, in the latter days thou shalt return to Jehovah thy God, and hearken unto his voice."

Important in this promise of restoration is the first reference to a time of special tribulation in the latter days which will be related to their return to their ancient land. This seems to be a reference to events which are yet future, connected with God's dealings with Israel in the time of trouble preceding the millennial kingdom.

One of the major sections in the Bible on Israel's sufferings is found in the closing chapters of Deuteronomy. After outlining the basis for blessing while they were in the land (Deuteronomy 28:1-14), Moses turns to the subject of God's chastening discipline upon them if they depart from His law. He points out that God will curse them and He will smite them with all types of afflictions and that ultimately they will be scattered over the face of the earth.

The closing verses of Deuteronomy 28, beginning with verse 62, are a graphic description of God's future discipline of the nation. Moses writes: "And ye shall be left few in number, whereas ye were as the stars of heaven for multitude; because thou didst not hearken unto the voice of Jehovah thy God. And it shall come to pass, that, as Jehovah rejoiced over you to do you good, and to multiply you, so Jehovah will rejoice over you to cause you to perish, and to destroy you; and ye shall be plucked from off the land whither thou goest in to possess it. And Jehovah will scatter thee among all peoples, from the one end of the earth even unto the other end of the earth; and there thou shalt serve other gods, which thou hast not known, thou nor thy fathers, even wood and stone. And among these nations shalt thou find no ease, and there shall be no rest for the sole of thy foot: but Jehovah will give thee there a trembling heart, and failing of eyes, and pining of soul;

and thy life shall hang in doubt before thee; and thou shalt fear night and day, and shalt have no assurance of thy life. In the morning thou shalt say, Would it were even! and at even thou shalt say, Would it were morning: for the fear of thy heart which thou shalt fear, and for the sight of thine eyes which thou shalt see" (Deuteronomy 28:62-67).

In this massive prediction of Israel's future sufferings, God makes plain that Israel will be left few in number, they will be scattered among all the nations of the earth, and they will have no rest of mind or heart, their very lives being in danger from morning until evening. The fearful consequences of neglecting the law have been only too graphically fulfilled in the history of the nation.

Recorded in the Old Testament itself are the captivities which were a major form of suffering for Israel. The ten tribes were carried off by the Assyrians in the eighth century B.C. This was followed by the captivity of Babylon in the seventh and sixth centuries B.C. Once again the land lay desolate, the beautiful city of Jerusalem was in ruins, and the evidences of God's loving favor were in a large measure erased. The divine judgment came only after centuries of warning not only in the written Word, but the oral ministry of prophets who plainly told the children of Israel of that which would beset them if they did not return to the Lord. The Old Testament, however, closes with Israel back in the land, re-established in their ancient cities, and once again worshiping at the temple of God.

In the New Testament after the four hundred years which separate the Old and New Testaments, the strain of prophecy concerning Israel's future sufferings is continued. With the gathering opposition of the religious leaders of the Jews as well as widespread defection among those who had originally followed Christ, the closing messages of Christ were messages of judgment. In the twenty-third chapter of Matthew, Christ solemnly pronounces divine judgment upon the scribes and the Pharisees: "Woe unto you, scribes and Pharisees, hypocrites! for ye build the sep-

ulchres of the prophets, and garnish the tombs of the righteous, and say, If we had been in the days of our fathers, we
should not have been partakers with them in the blood
of the prophets. Wherefore ye witness to yourselves, that
ye are the sons of them that slew the prophets. Fill ye
up then the measure of your fathers. Ye serpents, ye offspring of vipers, how shall ye escape the judgment of hell?
Therefore, behold, I send unto you prophets, and wise men,
and scribes: some of them shall ye kill and crucify; and some
of them shall ye scourge in your synagogues, and perse-
cute from city to city: that upon you may come all the
righteous blood shed on the earth, from the blood of Abel
the righteous unto the blood of Zachariah son of Barachiah,
whom ye slew between the sanctuary and the altar. Verily
I say unto you, All these things shall come upon this generation. O Jerusalem, Jerusalem, that killeth the prophets,
and stoneth them that are sent unto her! how often would
I have gathered thy children together, even as a hen gather-
eth her chickens under her wings, and ye would not! Behold, your house is left unto you desolate. For I say unto
you, Ye shall not see me henceforth, till ye shall say, Blessed
is he that cometh in the name of the Lord" (Matthew 23:
29-39).

In pronouncing judgment upon His generation, Christ
was in effect predicting the final dispersion and their ultimate regathering when the godly remnant of Israel in
repentance would say: "Blessed is he that cometh in the
name of the Lord." In the early portion of the twenty-fourth
chapter of Matthew the postscript to this prediction is
given. When the disciples came to show Christ the splendor
of the buildings of the temple, Christ answered: "See ye
not all these things? verily I say unto you, There shall not
be left here one stone upon another, that shall not be thrown
down" (Matthew 24:2). In reply to further questions from
His disciples, He predicted the course of the present age
including the dramatic prediction of Matthew 24:9: "Then
shall they deliver you up unto tribulation, and shall kill
you: and ye shall be hated of all the nations for my name's

sake." Like Moses of old, He solemnly warned the children of Israel. Christ, the prophet of whom Moses spoke, delivered a similar message to His generation much of which has already been fulfilled in the centuries since Christ. In A.D. 70 Jerusalem was destroyed and with it the magnificent temple. In the years that followed, Israel was the object of fearful persecution, culminating with the complete desecration of the land of Israel in A.D. 135 by the Roman soldiers. The sad condition of being scattered to the ends of the earth has persisted until the twentieth century, and with it has come untold sufferings to the people of Israel climaxing in the terrible scourge of Hitler who murdered some six million of the people of Israel. But, according to the prophets, the end is not yet and ahead of Israel is a terrible time of suffering before the day of restoration.

THE FUTURE TIME OF JACOB'S TROUBLE

The predictions of Israel's suffering as given in the Old and New Testaments, while fulfilled in part to the present hour, are yet to have their climax. As intimated as early as Deuteronomy 4, Israel is destined to have a particular time of suffering which will eclipse anything that it has known in the past. The Prophet Jeremiah gave an extensive revelation on this subject in the thirtieth chapter of his prophecy in connection with his prediction of the ultimate restoration of the people of Israel. A tragic picture of that future hour is given in Jeremiah 30:5-7: "For thus saith Jehovah: We have heard a voice of trembling, of fear, and not of peace. Ask ye now, and see whether a man doth travail with child: wherefore do I see every man with his hands on his loins, as a woman in travail, and all faces are turned into paleness? Alas! for that day is great, so that none is like it: it is even the time of Jacob's trouble; but he shall be saved out of it."

In Jeremiah's prophecy the main elements of Israel's future time of tribulation are unfolded. It is declared to be a time of great trouble which will be greater than any time of suffering in Israel's past. It will be peculiarly "the time

of Jacob's trouble" in that Israel will be singled out for
suffering in that day. Yet coupled with the prediction of
unprecedented tribulation is the prediction that "he shall
be saved out of it." The time of trouble is going to be climaxed by a time of deliverance when the prophecy given
in Jeremiah 30:3 is fulfilled: "For, lo, the days come, saith
Jehovah, that I will turn again the captivity of my people
Israel and Judah, saith Jehovah; and I will cause them to
return to the land that I gave to their fathers, and they shall
possess it."

The Prophet Daniel in a similar way refers to Israel's
time of trouble. After predicting the warfare which will
characterize the Middle East at the time of the end, Daniel
goes on to prophesy: "And at that time shall Michael stand
up, the great prince who standeth for the children of thy
people; and there shall be a time of trouble such as never
was since there was a nation even to that same time: and
at that time thy people shall be delivered, every one that
shall be found written in the book" (Daniel 12:1). Like
the prophecy of Jeremiah, Daniel predicted that the future
time of Israel's tribulation would surpass anything they had
ever known and that it would be climaxed by their deliverance.

The purge of Israel in their time of trouble is described
by Zechariah in these words: "And it shall come to pass,
that in all the land, saith Jehovah, two parts therein shall
be cut off and die; but the third shall be left therein. And
I will bring the third part into the fire, and will refine
them as silver is refined, and will try them as gold is tried"
(Zechariah 13:8, 9). According to Zechariah's prophecy,
two thirds of the children of Israel in the land will perish,
but the one third that are left will be refined and be awaiting the deliverance of God at the second coming of Christ
which is described in the next chapter of Zechariah.

On this same subject of Israel's coming time of suffering, Christ Himself delivered a dramatic prediction. In
the course of His prophetic message in Matthew 24, He
instructed the disciples: "When therefore ye see the abom-

ination of desolation, which was spoken of through Daniel the prophet, standing in the holy place (let him that readeth understand), then let them that are in Judaea flee unto the mountains: let him that is on the housetop not go down to take out the things that are in his house: and let him that is in the field not return back to take his cloak. But woe unto them that are with child and to them that give suck in those days! And pray ye that your flight be not in the winter, neither on a sabbath: for then shall be a great tribulation, such as hath not been from the beginning of the world until now, no, nor ever shall be. And except those days had been shortened, no flesh would have been saved, but for the elect's sake those days shall be shortened" (Matthew 24: 15-22).

In this passage Christ introduces the fact that the time of the great tribulation is going to be that of which Daniel the Prophet spoke in connection with his reference to the abomination of desolation. It seems clear that Christ had in mind the prediction of the climax of Israel's seventieth week or seventy sevens of years mentioned in Daniel 9:27. Here many expositors understand the passage to teach that the prince that shall come, the future Roman dictator mentioned in Daniel 9:26, will make a covenant with Israel for a period of seven years. This covenant, after running half its course, is broken in the middle of the seven years and Israel, instead of being a protected nation, becomes the object of fearful persecution.

We read of this in Daniel 9:27 in these words: "And he shall make a firm covenant with many for one week: and in the midst of the week he shall cause the sacrifice and the oblation to cease; and upon the wing of abominations shall come one that maketh desolate; and even unto the full end, and that determined, shall wrath be poured out upon the desolate." Further light on this abomination of desolation is given in Daniel 12:11 where it is predicted: "And from the time that the continual burnt-offering shall be taken away, and the abomination that maketh desolate set up, there shall be a thousand two hundred and ninety days." This apparently is a reference to the breaking of the covenant, the stopping of Jewish sacrifices, and the erection of an idol representing the prince that shall come who will become a world ruler.

In commenting on Daniel's prophecy, Christ exhorts those who are living in the day of its fulfillment in Judea to flee to the mountains, not bothering to get their ordinary possessions. It will be a time of special trial to those with small children and their flight will be made doubly difficult if it occurs in the winter, or in inclement weather, or on the Sabbath day when journeys are usually avoided and would therefore be conspicuous. Christ sums it up in Matthew 24:21, 22, in words that are reminiscent of Jeremiah and Daniel. He predicts that this period will be a time of great tribulation without parallel since the beginning of the world and will never be followed by a period of equal severity. He goes beyond the prophecies of Daniel and Jeremiah in His statement in verse 22: "And except those days had been shortened, no flesh would have been saved." In other words, the trials and difficulties of that day would be so severe that it would exterminate the entire human race if it were not for the fact that they are cut short by the return of Jesus Christ in power and glory to establish His kingdom. This future time of great tribulation is to be climactic in Israel's experience of suffering and is to be the final purging before God Himself interposes the judgments which begin the millennial kingdom.

The significance of Christ's statement that all flesh would perish unless the period were cut short is borne out by a study of this same period afforded in the book of the Revelation. Even a casual study of the description of the time of trouble which will characterize the end of the age will reveal a time of unprecedented difficulty.

As held by many expositors, the chronological structure of the book of Revelation is supplied by the sequence of seven seals affixed to the scroll in the possession of the Lamb. As each seal is broken, it unfolds a new period in the order of end-time events. The seventh seal is a comprehensive one, apparently including in its scope the details provided in the seven trumpets which subsequently sound and including the events described as the outpouring of seven bowls of the wrath of God which is related to the seventh trumpet.

The scene of devastation of divine judgment and human iniquity which is unfolded in these events is without parallel in the history of the world. According to Revelation 6:7, the judgments attending the opening of the fourth seal involve the death with sword, famine, and wild beasts of one fourth of the earth's population. If this were applied to the present world population now approaching three billion, it would mean that 750,000,000 people would perish, more than the total population of North America, Central America, and South America combined. It seems clear that this is only one of a series of gigantic catastrophes. In the judgments described as following the trumpets of the angels, a third part of the remaining population of the world is described as destroyed in Revelation 9:15. The concluding judgment proceeding from the seventh bowl of the wrath of God poured out on the earth in Revelation 16:17-21 is even more devastating than anything that had occurred previously. The stark reality of the words of Christ that the entire race would be blotted out if that period were not terminated by His return seems to be supported by these details.

Though the judgments will obviously fall on all races and people, it seems that Israel is to be the special object of satanic hatred. This is borne out in the prophecy concerning the woman with child in Revelation 12. The best explanation of this symbolic presentation is that the woman is Israel and the child is the Lord Jesus Christ. The dragon, representing Satan, is portrayed as being cast down to the earth in Revelation 12:13 and, realizing that his time is short, according to the Scripture, "he persecuted the woman that brought forth the man child" (Revelation 12:13). The Scriptures which follow indicate the unrelenting warfare

against the woman and her seed and only by divine intervention is partial protection afforded her.

Out of the total number of Israel, a representative group
of 144,000 are sealed and thereby protected from destruction in this period. In Revelation 7, they are enumerated
with their respective tribes. In Revelation 14, they are
depicted on Mount Zion with the Lamb at the close of the
tribulation, still intact and singing praises to the Lord. They
form therefore the core of the godly remnant which will
be awaiting Christ when He returns to set up His millennial kingdom.

ISRAEL'S DELIVERANCE FROM SUFFERING

Just as the Scriptures faithfully portray the fact of
Israel's suffering climaxing in the great tribulation, the
Word of God also promises deliverance at its close. This
was noted in all the great passages dealing with the subject, as in Deuteronomy 4, Jeremiah 30, Daniel 12, and
Matthew 24. Of special importance is the prediction given
by the Apostle Paul in Romans 11:25-27: "For I would not,
brethren, have you ignorant of this mystery, lest ye be
wise in your own conceits, that a hardening in part hath
befallen Israel, until the fulness of the Gentiles be come in;
and so all Israel shall be saved: even as it is written, There
shall come out of Zion the Deliverer; he shall turn away
ungodliness from Jacob: and this is my covenant unto them,
when I shall take away their sins." In this passage it is
predicted that the present age of fullness of blessings for
the Gentiles will pass and be succeeded by a restoration
to Israel. At that time Israel will be delivered, as indicated in the words: "And so all Israel shall be saved."

Though the meaning of this passage has been debated,
probably the best interpretation is to regard it as a national promise, namely, that at the time of the end when
her period of suffering has been fulfilled, Israel as a nation
or Israel as a whole shall be delivered from her enemies.
The salvation in view is not that of freedom from the guilt
of sin, but deliverance from persecution and trial. This

will be accomplished when the Deliverer comes out of Zion, an unmistakable reference to Jesus Christ. When He returns, He will come to the Mount of Olives. As depicted in Zechariah 14:4, He will establish His government in Jerusalem and from Zion will go forth the law. According to Isaiah 2:3: "And many peoples shall go and say, Come ye, and let us go up to the mountain of Jehovah, to the house of the God of Jacob; and he will teach us of his ways, and we will walk in his paths: for out of Zion shall go forth the law, and the word of Jehovah from Jerusalem." At that time God's covenant of blessing upon Israel will be fulfilled as embodied in the new covenant of Jeremiah 31 and mercy will be shown the people of Israel instead of the searching judgments of the tribulation period which have preceded.

In contemplating this tremendous revelation of God's divine purpose and plan for Israel, the Apostle Paul breaks forth in a doxology: "O the depth of the riches both of the wisdom and the knowledge of God! how unsearchable are his judgments and his ways past tracing out! For who hath known the mind of the Lord? or who hath been his counsellor? or who hath first given to him, and it shall be recompensed unto him again? For of him, and through him, and unto him, are all things. To him be the glory for ever. Amen" (Romans 11:33-36).

SUMMARY

The important world events which are taking place today may be regarded as a prelude to the consummation which will include Israel's time of suffering. Heart-rending as it may be to contemplate, the people of Israel who are returning to their ancient land are placing themselves within the vortex of this future whirlwind which will destroy the majority of those living in the land of Palestine. The searching and refining fire of divine judgment will produce in Israel that which is not there now, an attitude of true repentance and eager anticipation of the coming of their

Messiah. The tribulation period will then be followed by Israel's day of glory.

For the Christian these events are of utmost significance, for many Scriptures seem to teach that Christ will come for the church, the body of saints, in this present age of grace, before these end-time events take place. Israel's day of suffering will be preceded by the translation of the church and the resurrection of the dead in Christ. The swiftly moving events of our generation are not a basis for despair, but another reminder that God majestically fulfills His will. Every prophecy will find its counterpart in complete fulfillment, and the wisdom and mercy and sovereignty of God will be vindicated before all His creatures. Christ is not only the hope of Israel, but also the hope of all those who are trusting Him.

CHAPTER VII

THE GLORIOUS RESTORATION OF ISRAEL

The partial restoration of the nation Israel to their ancient land in the middle of the twentieth century should be recognized by all careful students of the Bible as a most remarkable event. It seems to be a token that God is about to fulfill His Word concerning the glorious future of His chosen people. As has been pointed out in previous discussion, the return of Israel to their ancient land and the establishment of the state of Israel is the first step in a sequence of events which will culminate in Christ's millennial kingdom on earth. The present return of Israel is the prelude and will be followed by the dark hour of their suffering in the great tribulation. This will in turn be succeeded by the return of Christ, the establishment of Christ's kingdom on earth, and the exaltation of the people of Israel to a place of prominence and blessing. Scriptures already discussed have brought out these major aspects of Israel's future program. This concluding study will concern itself with the fulfillment of countless prophecies relating to them in relationship to the millennial reign of Christ.

THE FINAL JUDGMENT OF ISRAEL

At the time of the second coming of Christ to establish His kingdom, two major aspects of Israel's judgment may be observed. First, the righteous dead of Israel will be raised and will be judged relative to rewards. Second, those in Israel who have survived the great tribulation will be judged, and the righteous in Israel will enter into the Promised Land and enjoy the blessings of the millennial kingdom.

115

The resurrection of the righteous of Israel is indicated in Daniel 12:2, 3 in these words: "And many of them that sleep in the dust of the earth shall awake, some to everlasting life, and some to shame and everlasting contempt. And they that are wise shall shine as the brightness of the firmament; and they that turn many to righteousness as the stars for ever and ever." Scholars have not all agreed on the details indicated by this prophecy. It has been characteristic of some branches of premillenarians to include the resurrection of Israel with the resurrection of the church at the time of the rapture. Those who have followed this interpretation have been somewhat embarrassed by the fact that Daniel 12:1, 2 seems to place the resurrection of Israel after the tribulation instead of before it. This would indicate either that the rapture is postribulational in that the resurrection follows the tribulation, or that they were wrong in their preliminary judgment that the resurrection of Israel occurred at the time of a pretribulational rapture.

Though disagreement on the interpretation of this passage continues, many careful students of premillennial truth have come to the conclusion that the opinion that Israel's resurrection occurred at the time of the rapture was a hasty one and without proper Scriptural foundation. It seems far more preferable to regard the resurrection of Daniel 12:2 as a literal one following the tribulation, but not to be identified with the pretribulational rapture of the church. If this interpretation be allowed, then the expression "many of them that sleep in the dust of the earth shall awake" can be regarded as a literal and bodily resurrection of righteous Israel from the grave in order that they might participate in the millennial reign of Christ as resurrected beings along with the resurrected and translated church of the New Testament.

A further difficulty is found in the fact that Daniel 12:2 states that some awake to everlasting life and "some to shame and everlasting contempt." Premillenarians are agreed that the resurrection of the wicked does not occur until after the thousand-year reign of Christ. The declaration of the resurrection of the righteous in almost the same breath as the resurrection of the wicked, separated as they are by the thousand-year reign of Christ, is a difficulty for some premillenarians.

A careful study of the passage, however, reveals that most of the difficulty is in the English translation. The Hebrew seems to make quite a sharp contrast between those who are raised to everlasting life and those who are raised to shame and everlasting contempt. A paraphrase would render the passage this way: "Many of them that sleep in the dust of the earth shall awake, these to everlasting life, and those to shame and everlasting contempt." The passage then becomes a statement that subsequent to the tribulation all the dead will be raised, but in two groups, one group to everlasting life and the other group to everlasting contempt. The fact that these are separated in time is clearly spelled out in Revelation 20, and the fact that this detail is not given here should not be considered a major problem.

It is evident from Daniel 12:3 that the main purpose of this revelation is to deal with the resurrection of the wise. These are declared to "shine as the brightness of the firmament; and they that turn many to righteousness as the stars for ever and ever." In this statement it is evident that the resurrected saints of the Old Testament, which is primarily the resurrection of Israel but will undoubtedly include the righteous of the Gentiles as well, will be an occasion for recognition of their good works. Rewards will be distributed to them much in the way that rewards were given to the church, that is, those who are righteous will be given places of prominence and privilege in the millennial kingdom of Christ and their righteousness will be displayed for all to see.

A parallel passage to this resurrection of Israel from the dead is found in Isaiah 26:14, 19. Verse 14 says: "They are dead, they shall not live; they are deceased, they shall not rise: therefore hast thou visited and destroyed them, and made all remembrance of them to perish." In contrast to the wicked whose end is here described as not being included in the resurrection of the righteous, the prospect of Israel is declared in verse 19: "Thy dead shall live; my dead bodies shall arise. Awake and sing, ye that dwell in the dust; for thy dew is as the dew of herbs, and the earth shall cast forth the dead." Though perhaps less clear than the Daniel 12 reference, Isaiah 26 confirms the idea of the resurrection of the righteous dead in Israel. It may be concluded that at the beginning of the millennium all of the righteous dead have been raised. The church will be raised at the time of the rapture before the tribulation, and Old Testament saints, including Israel, at the beginning of the millennial reign of Christ. Only the wicked dead remain in the graves awaiting their resurrection at the end of the millennial kingdom.

Those in Israel who survive the tribulation and who are on earth at the time of Christ's second coming are declared to be judged in Ezekiel 20:34-38. Ezekiel states: "And I will bring you out from the peoples, and will gather you out of the countries wherein ye are scattered, with a mighty hand, and with an outstretched arm, and with wrath poured out; and I will bring you into the wilderness of the peoples, and there will I enter into judgment with you face to face. Like as I entered into judgment with your fathers in the wilderness of the land of Egypt, so will I enter into judgment with you, saith the Lord Jehovah. And I will cause you to pass under the rod, and I will bring you into the bond of the covenant; and I will purge out from among you the rebels, and them that transgress against me; I will bring them forth out of the land where they sojourn, but they shall not enter into the land of Israel: and ye shall know that I am Jehovah."

As in previous declarations concerning God's work of restoring Israel at the beginning of the millennial kingdom, the judgment of Israel is preceded by their regathering from all the peoples of the earth. They are assembled in the place described as "the wilderness of the peoples" and there God declares that He will enter into judgment upon them. It will be like the judgment of their forefathers at the time of the Exodus when the adult population perished in the forty years of wandering, but the younger generation was permitted to enter into the land. In this judgment of living Israel at the beginning of the millennial kingdom, God says that He will have them pass under the rod and that He will purge out the unrighteous described as "the rebels" and as "them that transgress against me." Though included in the work of regathering, they will not enter into the Promised Land and apparently perish like their gainsaying forefathers in the wilderness.

The clearcut division in Israel of those who are righteous and those who are unrighteous arises from the fact that some are saved by faith in Christ, but others rejected Him and were worshipers of the beast, the world ruler of the great tribulation. According to Revelation 13:8 all those on earth during the great tribulation will worship the world ruler except for those whose names are written in the book of life. It is stated in Revelation 14:9 that those who are worshipers of the beast come under the fearful wrath of God and are cast into everlasting torment forever and ever. A similar conclusion is derived from the parable of the wheat and the tares in Matthew 13 where all the tares are burned up and the wheat is gathered into the barn. Israel's purging judgment at the end of the age will therefore not only include the trials of the great tribulation in which two thirds of the nation will perish, but will culminate in the judgment of God following their regathering in which all unbelievers who remain will be purged out. The millennial kingdom, therefore, will begin with the godly remnant of Israel who have put their trust in the Lord and who will desire to follow the leadership of their Messiah and King.

THE RULE OF CHRIST OVER ISRAEL

According to the second Psalm, it is the divine purpose of God that His Son will reign over the earth. In spite of the raging of the nations and their rebellion against God, the sovereign purpose of God that His Son will rule is plainly stated in these words: "Yet I have set my king upon my holy hill of Zion. I will tell of the decree: Jehovah said unto me, Thou art my son; this day have I begotten thee. Ask of me, and I will give thee the nations for thine inheritance, and the uttermost parts of the earth for thy possession. Thou shalt break them with a rod of iron; thou shalt dash them in pieces like a potter's vessel" (Psalm 2:6-9). In this declaration God not only affirms that Christ will reign from Mount Zion, but that all the nations of the world will come under His reign. It will be an absolute government as shown in the expression: "Thou shalt break them with a rod of iron; thou shalt dash them in pieces like a potter's vessel."

The rule of the Son of God is described in a similar way in many other passages. In Daniel 7:13, 14 it is written: "I saw in the night-visions, and, behold, there came with the clouds of heaven one like unto a son of man, and he came even to the ancient of days, and they brought him near before him. And there was given him dominion, and glory, and a kingdom, that all the peoples, nations, and languages should serve him: his dominion is an everlasting dominion, which shall not pass away, and his kingdom that which shall not be destroyed." Here the kingdom is described, not simply in its millennial context, but as that which continues after the millennium in the eternal state.

According to Isaiah 2:1-4, Jerusalem will be the center of the millennial government. Beginning in verse 2 Isaiah writes: "And it shall come to pass in the latter days, that the mountain of Jehovah's house shall be established on the top of the mountains, and shall be exalted above the hills; and all nations shall flow unto it. And many peoples shall go and say, Come ye, and let us go up to the mountain of Jehovah, to the house of the God of Jacob; and he will teach us of his ways, and we will walk in his paths: for out of Zion shall go forth the law, and the word of Jehovah from Jerusalem. And he will judge between the nations,

and will decide concerning many peoples; and they shall
beat their swords into plowshares, and their spears into
pruning-hooks; nation shall not lift up sword against nation,
neither shall they learn war any more" (Isaiah 2:2-4).
From this passage it is evident that Jerusalem is to be the
capitol of the world, that from Zion the law will go forth,
and all nations will be under the sway of this righteous
government. The result will be that "they shall beat their
swords into plowshares, and their spears into pruning-hooks;
nation shall not lift up sword against nation, neither shall
they learn war any more" (Isaiah 2:4).

One of the interesting aspects of the millennial government is the fact that resurrected David will apparently
be a prince under Christ in administering the millennial
kingdom in so far as it relates to Israel. According to Ezekiel,
David will act as a shepherd over the people of Israel:
"And I will set up one shepherd over them, and he shall
feed them, even my servant David; he shall feed them,
and he shall be their shepherd. And I, Jehovah, will be
their God, and my servant David prince among them; I,
Jehovah, have spoken it" (Ezekiel 34:23, 24). Some have
interpreted this mention of David as a reference to Christ.
However, there is no good reason for not taking it in its
ordinary literal sense inasmuch as David will certainly be
raised from the dead and will be on the scene. What would
be more natural than to assign him a responsible place in
the government of Christ in relation to the people of Israel?
The concept that David will rule under Christ is found
not only here, but also in Jeremiah 30:9; 33:15-17; Ezekiel
37:24, 25; Hosea 3:5; and oblique references in Isaiah 55:
3, 4 and Amos 9:11.

The government of Christ will obviously be one of
righteousness and justice. In the comprehensive view of
the kingdom afforded in the prophecy of Isaiah 11:1-10,
the character of Christ's rule is revealed. In verses 3 to 5
the following description is given: "And his delight shall be
in the fear of Jehovah; and he shall not judge after the sight
of his eyes, neither decide after the hearing of his ears; but

with righteousness shall he judge the poor, and decide with equity for the meek of the earth; and he shall smite the earth with the rod of his mouth; and with the breath of his lips shall he slay the wicked. And righteousness shall be the girdle of his waist, and faithfulness the girdle of his loins." The millennial kingdom will therefore be a time of justice for all, and any who dare to rebel against the king will be subject to immediate divine judgment. For the first time since Adam the entire earth will be under the immediate control and direction of God with resulting blessing in every aspect of human life.

GENERAL CHARACTERISTICS OF THE MILLENNIAL KINGDOM

Students of prophecies relating to the millennial kingdom are embarrassed by the wealth of materials which is afforded. Passage after passage describes in glowing character the righteousness of the kingdom, the universal peace which will characterize the world, and the fact that there will be universal knowledge of the Lord. Peacefulness will not only extend to relationships of men, but even the natural world will be affected. Beasts that are naturally ferocious and enemies of other beasts will live together harmoniously. As depicted in Isaiah 11:6-9, it will be a time of universal knowledge of the Lord. According to Isaiah 11:9; "The earth shall be full of the knowledge of Jehovah, as the waters cover the sea." According to the provisions of the new covenant outlined by Jeremiah 31: 33, 34, God will write the law in the hearts of Israel and all will know the Lord. Jeremiah expresses this in these words: "But this is the covenant that I will make with the house of Israel after those days, saith Jehovah: I will put my law in their inward parts, and in their heart will I write it; and I will be their God, and they shall be my people. And they shall teach no more every man his brother saying, Know Jehovah; for they shall all know me, from the least of them unto the greatest of them, saith Jehovah: for I will forgive their iniquity, and their sin will I remember no more." It should be quite obvious that this is not a situ-

ation which exists today and in no literal sense are these
millennial prophecies being fulfilled now. This could only
be possible under the peculiar circumstances of the universal reign of Christ, the purging out of unbelievers at the
beginning of the millennium, and the constant proclamation
of the truth regarding Christ.

Many other passages confirm these conclusions. Isaiah
9:6, 7 affirms that Christ is the Prince of Peace who will
reign on the throne of David and establish justice and righteousness. Isaiah 16:5 reveals that Christ will sit in the tent
of David ministering perfect justice. Isaiah 24:23 states
that Jehovah of hosts will reign in Mount Zion. Isaiah
32:1 predicts that a king will administer absolute righteousness. Isaiah 40:1-11 is a classic passage predicting the coming of the King, climaxing its revelation in verses 10 and 11:
"Behold, the Lord Jehovah will come as a mighty one, and
his arm will rule for him: behold, his reward is with him,
and his recompense before him. He will feed his flock like
a shepherd, he will gather the lambs in his arm, and carry
them in his bosom, and will gently lead those that have
their young."

The ministry of Christ as King will not only be one of absolute justice, but one of great beneficence, as is brought
out in Isaiah 42:3, 4. According to Isaiah 52:7-15, the introduction to the great Messianic chapter, Isaiah 53, the
King will come to Zion. The kingdom which shall never
be destroyed will be set up by God, according to Daniel
2:44, and Christ's kingdom is declared to be everlasting
in Daniel 7:27. The prophecy of Micah 4:1-8 is similar to
that found in Isaiah 2. Micah 5:2-5 predicts the birth of
Christ in Bethlehem as One who is to be ruler in Israel
and who shall "be great unto the ends of the earth." The
familiar prophecy of Zechariah 9:9, quoted as fulfilled in
Matthew 21:5, pictures the King in His first coming, but
anticipates that "his dominion shall be from sea to sea, and
from the River to the ends of the earth" (Zechariah 9:10).

The concluding prediction of Zechariah 14:16, 17 gives
us an insight into the character of the millennial reign of

Christ. Zechariah writes: "And it shall come to pass, that every one that is left of all the nations that came against Jerusalem shall go up from year to year to worship the King, Jehovah of hosts, and to keep the feast of tabernacles. And it shall be, that whoso of all the families of the earth goeth not up unto Jerusalem to worship the King, Jehovah of hosts, upon them there shall be no rain." It is evident from this Scripture that Christ actively rules, requires the nations of the world to conform to His rule, and observe the religious rites which characterize the millennial kingdom. Taking the whole picture as provided by the prophets, the millennial kingdom depicts a world situation of righteousness, peace, and knowledge of the Lord which is quite foreign to the present age, but which will be subject to literal fulfillment when Christ actually reigns on earth.

ISRAEL'S SPIRITUAL LIFE IN THE MILLENNIUM

The very fact that Christ will be bodily and gloriously present in the earth during the millennial kingdom and that Satan will be bound and inactive (Revelation 20:1-3) provides a context of spiritual life on the part of Israel which is most favorable. As has been previously pointed out, everyone will have the basic facts about the Lord (Isaiah 11:9; Jeremiah 31:33, 34). The millennial government will assure that there will be peace among nations and righteousness in the administration of justice in relation to the individual (Isaiah 2:4; 11:3-5). The resulting world situation will be a joyous one in sharp contrast to the dark hour of Israel's suffering in the tribulation and her bitter experiences of centuries of wandering. Isaiah speaks of the joy of the Lord in that day in these words: "And in that day thou shalt say, I will give thanks unto thee, O Jehovah; for though thou wast angry with me, thine anger is turned away, and thou comfortest me. Behold, God is my salvation; I will trust, and will not be afraid: for Jehovah, even Jehovah, is my strength and song; and he is become my salvation. Therefore with joy shall ye draw water out of the wells of salvation" (Isaiah 12:1-3). Joy and gladness will

be as common as sighings and sadness were in Israel's
earlier experience.

The millennial period for both Israel and the Gentiles
will also be a time of special ministry of the Holy Spirit.
In this period, according to Isaiah 32:15, the Spirit will be
poured out from on high. A similar prophecy is found in
Isaiah 44:3: "For I will pour water upon him that is thirsty,
and streams upon the dry ground; I will pour my Spirit upon
thy seed, and my blessing upon thine offspring." Ezekiel
predicts: "And I will put my Spirit within you, and cause you
to walk in my statutes, and ye shall keep mine ordinances,
and do them" (Ezekiel 36:27). In Ezekiel 39:29 a further
similar statement is found: "Neither will I hide my face any
more from them; for I have poured out my Spirit upon the
house of Israel, saith the Lord Jehovah." The presence
of Christ, the evident power of the Holy Spirit, and the context of the knowledge of the Lord and peace, righteousness,
and joy will provide a basis for spiritual life in the millennium far more favorable than any preceding dispensation.

A number of Scriptures also describe the temple worship which will characterize the millennial kingdom. According to Ezekiel, a magnificent temple will be built, and
a system of priesthood and memorial sacrifices will be set
up. Scholars have not all agreed as to the interpretation
of this difficult portion of Ezekiel. Some have felt it impossible to have a system of animal sacrifices subsequent
to the one sacrifice of Christ on the cross in the light of
New Testament passages stating that the sacrifice of Christ
makes other sacrifices unnecessary. Though varied explana-
tions have been given for Ezekiel 40-48 which unfolds these
details, no satisfactory explanation has been made other
than that it is a description of millennial worship. In any
case, it is clear that the sacrifices are not expiatory, but merely
memorials of the one complete sacrifice of Christ. If in
the wisdom and sovereign pleasure of God the detailed
system of sacrifices in the Old Testament were a suitable
foreshadowing of that which would be accomplished by
the death of His Son, and if a memorial of Christ's death

is to be enacted, it would seem not unfitting that some sort of a sacrificial system would be used. While problems remain, it seems clear that Israel will have an ordered worship with Jerusalem once again the center of their religious as well as political life. A new order of priesthood would be required somewhat different than the Aaronic order, and rituals will be observed similar to the Mosaic order but differing in many aspects. In any case, a spiritual life of wonderful depth and reality far beyond anything Israel had known in her entire history will characterize her experience in the millennial kingdom. There will be complete fulfillment of Joel 2:28, 29 and blessings unmeasured will extend throughout the entire kingdom period.

SOCIAL, ECONOMIC, AND PHYSICAL ASPECTS OF ISRAEL IN THE KINGDOM

The combination of righteous government and abundant spiritual life will issue in many practical results in the millennial kingdom, and Israel will enjoy a period of physical as well as spiritual prosperity. Universal justice and peace will provide a proper basis for economic development without the curse of military expenditures, injustice, or inequities. Evidence seems to point to the fact that at the beginning of the millennium all adults who are permitted to enter the kingdom will be saved. The probability is that as children grow to maturity and a new generation is born a majority of those on the earth will experience real salvation, a situation far different than any previous period since the early days of man on earth. The curse inflicted upon the earth as a result of Adam's sin seems to be lifted, at least in part, during the millennial kingdom. Isaiah records the happy situation in Isaiah 35:1, 2: "The wilderness and the dry land shall be glad; and the desert shall rejoice, and blossom as the rose. It shall blossom abundantly, and rejoice even with joy and singing; the glory of Lebanon shall be given unto it, the excellency of Carmel and Sharon: they shall see the glory of Jehovah, the excellency of our God." As a result, the earth will bring forth in abundance and desert places formerly unproductive will have rich vegetation. There will be rainfall in areas where before there was drought (Isaiah 30:23; 35:7). Not only crops but cattle will prosper (Isaiah 30:23, 24).

There will be general prosperity in all aspects of economic development. Jeremiah speaks of this in Jeremiah 31:12: "And they shall come and sing in the height of Zion, and shall flow unto the goodness of Jehovah, to the grain, and to the new wine, and to the oil, and to the young of the flock and of the herd: and their soul shall be as a watered garden; and they shall not sorrow any more at all." Ezekiel speaks of causing evil beasts to depart out of the land, permitting them to sleep safely in the woods at night (Ezekiel 34:25). Increased rainfall is mentioned and abundant yielding of fruit trees (Ezekiel 34:26, 27). A similar picture is given in the prophecies of Joel 2:21-27. Joel writes of rich pastures, trees bearing fruit, and the vine yielding its strength, of rain coming down in abundance, of floors being full of wheat, of vats overflowing with wine, and Israel enjoying plenty of all the good things of the land. Amos gives a similar picture in the closing two verses of his book: "And I will bring back the captivity of my people Israel, and they shall build the waste cities, and inhabit them; and they shall plant vineyards, and drink the wine thereof; they shall also make gardens, and eat the fruit of them. And I will plant them upon their land, and they shall no more be plucked up out of their land which I have given them, saith Jehovah thy God" (Amos 9:14, 15).

Israel's experience in the millennium will also be one of physical health and freedom from disease. Isaiah 35:5, 6 seems to speak of this: "Then the eyes of the blind shall be opened, and the ears of the deaf shall be unstopped. Then shall the lame man leap as a hart, and the tongue of the dumb shall sing; for in the wilderness shall waters break out, and streams in the desert." In Isaiah 33:24 it is predicted: "And the inhabitant shall not say, I am sick: the people that dwell therein shall be forgiven their iniquity." A similar description of healing is given in Isaiah 29:18.

It would seem clear from prophecy that most of the earth's population will perish in the great tribulation and subsequent judgments and that the millennial kingdom begins with a comparatively small number of people. According to Jeremiah 30:19, 20, however, the earth's population will mushroom during the millennium and from those who have survived the tribulation who are still in their natural bodies, a multiplied offspring will come. According to Jeremiah 30:19, 20 God declares: "And I will multiply them, and they shall not be few; I will also glorify them, and they shall not be small. Their children also shall be as aforetime, and their congregation shall be established before me; and I will punish all that oppress them."

THE CONCLUSION OF THE MILLENNIAL KINGDOM

This selective study of the many Scriptures bearing upon the future restoration of Israel in the millennial kingdom of Christ constitutes a convincing demonstration of the glories of this period. Nothing comparable to this has ever been experienced in the history of man. It would seem that in the closing dispensation prior to the eternal state God is erecting the most favorable possible circumstances to which man could be subjected. When Satan is loosed again according to Revelation 20:7-9, how sad is the record that many born in the ideal circumstances of the millennium are revealed to have only outward profession and not real faith and submission to Christ. Once again judgment must fall upon those who have spurned every possible help in bringing them into proper relationship to their Lord and Saviour. The glorious millennial reign will be the capstone of Israel's history. Though the evidence seems to indicate that Israel will continue as a people into eternity, the millennium will be the final chapter of their history in the present earth. To this consummation the world is rapidly moving and the predicted sequence of events will unfold in proper succession once the present age has come to its close with the rapture of the church.

ISRAEL'S RESTORATION IN RELATION TO THE HOPE OF THE CHURCH

In the present world scene there are many indications pointing to the conclusion that the end of the age may soon be upon us. These prophecies relating to Israel's coming day of suffering and ultimate restoration may be destined for fulfillment in the present generation. Never before in the history of the world has there been a confluence of major evidences of preparation for the end.

Today, to the north of the nation Israel is the armed might of Russia. Never before has it seemed more likely that the prediction will be fulfilled given by Ezekiel (chapters 38 and 39) of an invasion from the north. To the east is the rising might of Red China, with the growing force of nationalism in India as well as the revival of Japan. Never before has it seemed more likely that there should be a tremendous military host coming from Asia, crossing the Euphrates river, and moving down on the scene of battle in the Middle East as predicted in Revelation 9:16.

The formation of the United Nations and the universal recognition of some form of world government as an alternative to war seem to be paving the way for the acceptance of the world ruler of Revelation 13 which will characterize the great tribulation. Never before have more people been persuaded that a world government is the only way to world peace.

The rising might of communism, embracing as it has a large portion of the world, and its spectacular rise which is without parallel in the history of the world, also has its prophetic portent. Though communism as such does not seem to enter into the prophetic picture of the end, its basic philosophy of materialistic atheism seems to be precisely the character of the false religion of the great tribulation (Daniel 11:36-38). Millions of youths in communistic lands are being systematically taught to trust only military might and to give blind allegiance to a human leader in place of worship of and service to the omnipotent

God. Just such a point of view and just such blind devotion will be required by the world ruler who will honor
only the god of military might and disregard all other
deities.

The modern movement toward a world church embodied in the ecumenical program seems also a preparation for acceptance by the world of a world church in the
earlier phases of the tribulation period. The wicked woman
of Revelation 17, the epitome of apostate ecclesiasticism,
seems to be the representation of this ultimate ecclesiastical
organization after every true Christian is removed by the
rapture. The apostasy and unbelief which exists in our
day seems to be the forerunner of the utter blasphemy
which will characterize the worship of the beast in Revelation 13.

One of the most dramatic evidences that the end of the
age is approaching is the fact that Israel has re-established
her position as a nation in her ancient land. Israel today
is in the proper place to enter into the covenant anticipated
in Daniel 9:27 which will begin the last seven-year period
leading up to the second coming of Christ. Even the
modern city of Jerusalem built by Israel is occupying the
precise area predicted in Jeremiah 31:38-40 and constitutes a fulfillment of this prophecy given twenty-five hundred years ago and never before fulfilled. Jeremiah states
that when Jerusalem is built in the area described, as it
has been in our generation, it will be a sign of the final
chapter in the history of Jerusalem, in preparation for the
millennial kingdom of our Lord.

The study of the history and prophecy of Israel is not
a mere academic exercise on the part of the theologian or
Bible student, but provides an unparalleled perspective of
the majestic dealings of God with this prophetic nation. In
it is revealed the faithfulness of God to the people whom
He sovereignly chose, the effective outworking of God's
wise purpose for them in spite of failure, delay, and
indifference to God's will. The fact that in our day there
is again movement and development in relation to this

ancient nation is a sign that the stage is being set for the final world drama. Certainly as Israel's promises are being fulfilled before our eyes other aspects of prophecy such as the resurrection of the dead in Christ and the translation of living saints become a real and an imminent possibility. The hope of Israel is also the hope of the church. With John the Apostle all faithful students of the prophetic Word can say: "Amen: come, Lord Jesus."

SELECTED BIBLIOGRAPHY

Allis, Oswald T., *Prophecy and the Church*. Philadelphia: The Presbyterian and Reformed Publishing Company, 1945.

Baron, David. *The History of Israel*. London: Morgan and Scott, Ltd., [n.d.].

Berkhof, Louis, *Systematic Theology*. Grand Rapids: Wm. B. Eerdmans Publishing Company, 1941.

Chafer, Lewis Sperry. *The Kingdom in History and Prophecy*. Findlay, Ohio: Dunham Publishing Company, 1919.

——. *Systematic Theology*, 8 vols. Dallas: Dallas Seminary Press, 1947.

DeHaan, M. R. *The Jew and Palestine in Prophecy*. Grand Rapids: Zondervan Publishing House, 1950.

Evans, Robert L. *The Jew and the Plan of God*. New York: Loizeaux Brothers, Inc., 1950.

Feinberg, Charles L. *Israel in the Spotlight*. Chicago: Scripture Press, 1956.

——. *Israel in the Last Days*. Altadena, California: Emeth Publications, 1953.

——. *Premillennialism or Amillennialism?* Fourth Edition. Wheaton: Van Kampen Press, 1954.

Hendriksen, William, *And So All Israel Shall Be Saved*. Grand Rapids: Baker Book Store, 1945.

Henry, Carl F. H. "The Christian Witness in Israel," *Christianity Today*, 5:22:22-23, August 14, 1961, 5:23:17-21, August 28, 1961.

——. "Israel: Marvel Among the Nations," *Christianity Today*, 5:24:13-16, September 11, 1961, 5:25:15-18, September 25, 1961.

——. "The Messianic Concept in Israel," *Christianity Today*, 6:1:7-12, October 13, 1961, 6:2:11-14, October 27, 1961.

Hodge, Charles, *Systematic Theology*. 3 vols. New York: Charles Scribner's Sons, 1887.

Kac, Arthur W. *The Rebirth of the State of Israel*. London: Marshall, Morgan, and Scott, Ltd., 1958.

Kligerman, Aaron J. *Messianic Prophecy in the Old Testament*. Grand Rapids: Zondervan Publishing House, 1957.

McClain, Alva J. *The Greatness of the Kingdom.* Grand Rapids: Zondervan Publishing House, 1959.

Murray, George L., *Millennial Studies.* Grand Rapids: Baker Book House, 1948.

Pentecost, J. Dwight. *Things to Come.* Findlay, Ohio: Dunham Publishing Company, 1958.

Peters, George N. H., *The Theocratic Kingdom.* 3 vols. Grand Rapids: Kregel Publications, 1952.

Pieters, Albertus. *The Seed of Abraham.* Grand Rapids: Wm. B. Eerdmans Publishing Company, 1950.

Pocket Guide to Middle East Questions. New York: The American Jewish Committee.

Ryrie, Charles C., *The Basis of the Premillennial Faith.* New York: Loizeaux Brothers, 1953.

Sale-Harrison, L. *The Remarkable Jew.* New York: Sale-Harrison Publications, 1934.

Saphir, Adolph. *Christ and Israel.* London: Morgan and Scott, Ltd., [n.d.].

Smith, Wilbur. *World Crisis in the Light of Prophetic Scriptures.* Chicago: Moody Press, 1951.

Thorbecke, Ellen. *Promised Land.* New York: Harper and Brothers, 1947.

Urquhart, John. *The Wonders of Prophecy.* Harrisburg, Pennsylvania: Christian Publications, Inc., [n.d.].

Vilnay, Z. *Israel Guide.* Jerusalem: Ahieber, 1961.

Walvoord, John F. *The Millennial Kingdom.* Findlay, Ohio: Dunham Publishing Company, 1959.

Wilkinson, John. *God's Plan for the Jew.* London: Mildnay Mission to the Jew, 1944.

———. *Israel, My Glory.* London: Mildnay Mission to the Jew Bookstore, 1894.

Wilkinson, Samuel H. *The Israel Promises and Their Fulfillment.* London: John Bale, Sons and Danielsson, Ltd., 1936.

TOPICAL INDEX

Abraham, continuance of his seed, 47, 48; eternal faith of, 40; failure to possess the land, 15; liberal denial of his historicity, 47; migration to the land, 15.

Abrahamic covenant, 27-45; amillennial exegesis of, 38-42; as conditional in amillennial theology, 40-43; as everlasting, 48; as unconditional, 40-44; Gentile blessing, 36-38; interpreted literally, 34-40; requirement of circumcision, 43; summary, 33, 34, 44, 45.

Agriculture, of Israel, 21, 22.

Alexander the Great, conquest of Palestine, 17.

Allis, Oswald, on Israel in New Testament, 56; view of Abrahamic covenant, 41-43; view of new covenant, 54, 55.

Angels, eschatology of, 28.

Apostasy, 130.

Army, of Israel, 20, 21.

Asia, in prophecy, 129.

Captivities, of Israel, 16.

Chafer, L. S., interpretation of new covenant, 53, 54.

Christ, government in the millennium, 119-22; rule over Gentiles, 119-20; rule over Israel, 119-22.

Church, eschatology of, 28.

Circumcision, in relation to the Abrahamic covenant, 43.

Cities, of Israel, 23.

Communism, 129.

Constitution, of Israel, 20.

Covenant theology, 29, 30.

David, prince of the millennial kingdom, 121; promise of the kingdom to, 80-100.

Davidic covenant, 80-100 (see Kingdom, Davidic).

Dispersion of Israel, by Romans, 17; followed by regatherings, 72-74.

Ecumenical movement, 130.

Educational system, of Israel, 23, 24.

End of the age impending, 129-131.

Eschatology, definition of, 27; four major divisions, 28; modern concept, 27; principle of organization, 28; program for angels, 28; program for Gentiles, 28; program for Israel, 28; program for the church, 28.

Eternal state, in Abraham's faith, 40.

Exodus, from Egypt to the Promised Land, 15, 16.

Gentiles, as Seed of Abraham, 36-38; eschatology of, 28.

Government, of Israel, 20; world, 129.

Hebrew, revival of, 23, 24.

Hendriksen, William, on Israel in the New Testament, 56; on Israel's future, 46.

Herzl, Theodor, 15.

History, of Israel in the Old Testament, 15; proof of continuance, 47, 48.

Hodge, Charles, on Israel in New Testament, 56; on Israel's future, 46.

Industry, of Israel, 23.

Interpretation, Augustinian principle of, 30, 31; principles of Biblical, 30, 31.

Israel, as seed of Abraham, 36-38; contrasted to church, 55-59; contrasted to church by recent amillenarians, 55, 56; contrasted to Gentiles, 56; deliverance from future sufferings, 112, 113; denial of future, 46; eschatology in its covenants, 28; final judgment, 115-19; fulfillment of prophecy of suffering, 103-7; future as a nation, summary, 61, 62; future of, 46-62; 101-31; future restoration, 115-31; future suffering, predicted by Christ, 105-7; future time of suffering, 101-14; future time of suffering, causes, 101-3; God's faithfulness to, 102, 103; in eternity, 128; in great tribulation, 106, 107; in millennium, 98, 99; in relation to Davidic kingdom, 97, 98; in tribulation, 97, 98; postmillennial concept of future, 46; regathering of, 66-71; restoration to land, 130; resurrection, 116-18; resurrection before tribulation, 116-18; rule of Christ over, 119-22; satanic opposition, 101-3; suffering, in the book of Revelation, 108-12; sufferings, summary, 113, 114; war with Arabs, 19.

Jerusalem, capitol of millennial kingdom, 120, 121; modern city of, 130.

Judgment, of Israel, 115-19.

Kingdom, Davidic, amillennial interpretation, 96; argument of Peters,

INDEX TO SCRIPTURES